Circle of Frith:

A Devotional to Frigg and Her Handmaidens

Frigg and her maidens, as envisioned in Wägner and MacDowell,
Asgard and the Gods (1886)

Circle of Frith:

A Devotional to Frigg and Her Handmaidens

By Rev. Maire Durkan

The Troth

2021

Published by The Troth
325 Chestnut Street, Suite 800
Philadelphia, PA 19106
http://www.thetroth.org/

ISBN-13: 978-1-941136-43-0 (hardcover)
978-1-941136-44-7 (paperback)
978-1-941136-45-4 (PDF)
978-1-941136-46-1 (EPUB)
978-1-941136-47-8 (MOBI)

Troth logo designed by Kveldúlfr Gundarsson; drawn by 13 Labs, Chicago, Illinois
Typeset in Junicode 12

Cover art: Erin Durkan
Cover design: Ben Waggoner

There, in the glen, Fensaler stands, the house
Of Frea, honored mother of the gods,
And shows its lighted windows to the main.

Balder Dead by Matthew Arnold

Hail and welcome to my circle of frith!

Syn opens the door to my realm.

Come, sit by my hearth!

My ladies and I will spin and weave,

shaping magic, stories, desires, deeds, and oaths

into the web of wyrd.

My regal ladies hold my light and favor

responsible rulers of their realms

of being and doing.

As you are here, you too have work to do!

Come and join us

Forge new friendships

Learn of our crafts!

Frigg's Invitation by Maire Durkan

Contents

Frigg as envisioned in Sander,
Edda Sämund den Vises (1893)

Introduction

I sit at my kitchen table on an astonishingly quiet and serene Friday—Frigg's Day—morning, with a mug of strong Irish tea on one side of my laptop and a statue of Frigg and copious books and notebooks on the other. My house is almost never this quiet. In a world where few folk, including all of my adult children and their partners, consider having large families, I'm a bit of a dinosaur with nine children ranging in age from 14 to 34. As our four youngest still live here and their friends and our friends are over often, our home is usually filled with noisy, buoyant energy. Meals, celebrations, rituals, and general hanging out happen regularly under this roof and in our yard. Friends, family, and guests are all welcome here.

That being said, I'm also a Friggswoman. Although my lifestyle (i.e. monogamous, married, cisgendered, white female) is hardly breaking news, being a witch and a Heathen puts a bit of a spin on that narrative. But Frigg is a goddess for *everyone,* and the qualities that make Her who She is can support and encourage the spiritual and mundane aspects of our lives, regardless of gender identification, ethnicity, age, or ability. Frigg is like us, in that She, too, wears many hats and has many responsibilities and can't be defined by one role. In a microcosmic sense, like Frigg, I am the mother of many, and like Her, my life and my evolution encompass many other roles and responsibilities that are just as essential and that define who and what I am in this incarnation.

Like Frigg, we all delegate some of these responsibilities to others. In my case, Frigg has her handmaidens; I have my kids! A key phrase that Frigg has inserted into my consciousness on more than one occasion is, "Do what you can with the time that you have." Although She exists outside of time and I'm as finite and mortal as can be, we both "get" the necessity of doing what we can with the time that we have. Sometimes, regardless of our life's journey, we are all overwhelmed by our mountain of duties, obligations, plans, and longings. In her quiet, firm, yet loving way, Frigg will tell you to get over yourself and get on with the tasks at hand—multi-tasking or one by one (for Her it's multi-tasking). Even a goddess with the blessing and burden of foreknowledge works this way—and if she is your *fulltrúa* (fully trusted one), you better get with the program.

If you are new to Heathenry, Ásatrú, and the northern pantheons of gods and goddesses, the Æsir and Ásynjur, your only experience of Frigg (also anglicized as Frigga) may be through Marvel's comics and movies which, although entertaining, are not the least bit faithful to the actual lore. While I bet that Loki was tickled to be portrayed as her adopted son, Marvel is hardly an accurate source of information on the gods and goddesses or the Nine Worlds. However, Marvel comics may have been the spark that led you here and to a wonderful spiritual journey. Frigg would approve of that.

If she is neither Marvel's version, nor Wagner's bitchy vindictive wife, Fricka, who "whirls the whip. . . wrath in her look," who is She? That question will be answered a bit differently by each person who experiences Her energy. But there are traits that have been reported over time.

Organized, focused, determined, creative, compassionate, empathetic, wise, shrewd, and *powerful* are some of the adjectives that I equate with Frigg as I experience Her here and now. As you will discover as we examine Frigg in the Lore, she is and always has been all of these things and much more. She is a mother, the All-Mother, and that role is certainly one at which she excels, but she is also lady of the keep and of the *innangard* (our kin of blood and spirit and our home place. . . it's bigger than that, so check out other sources, including The Troth's *Our Troth* volumes). To continue the extended metaphor, if Odin is the Chairman of Asgard, Frigg is its CEO. She communicates and listens, builds frithful relationships, is realistic, and willing to take calculated risks. She can also read her associates and employees (in many realms) well and adapts her management style to the necessary time and place when She deals with humans. Of course, because she is also a seer with foreknowledge, we can add foreknowledge to that list!

Some of my other hats include ordained godperson for The Troth and my larger Heathen and Pagan communities, children's book writer, birth and postpartum doula, and witch and bonded member of Grail of the Birch Moon in the Assembly of the Sacred Wheel tradition. As a fantasy writer with a northern twist, I began researching Norse lore in the early 2000s. (I grew up with *D'Aulaires' Book of Norse Myths* and Astrid Lindgren's *The Tomten*, so my imagination was primed thanks to my father's reading choices.) Those were probably my first steps along this path and, although I didn't realize this fully at the time, I was definitely being called, first by Freyja and Odin, and later (and more quietly but firmly) by Frigg. It was Frigg who led me to The Troth and to its Lore and Clergy programs. Towards the end of my first year in the Lore program, I had what you might call a UPG from my *fulltrúa*, Frigg, that I should expand my role as a frith builder and become Heathen clergy. Although I honor the gods and goddesses that are celebrated in my Assembly work (we also honor the Norse pantheon), Heathenry is the path of my heart. Odin and Freya first called to me through my writing, but it is Frigg who best suits me, and I believe that I suit her purposes as well.

Because we live in a world where loathsome hate groups abuse our sacred symbols and our gods, I will continue to express and share the Troth's inclusive faith tradition. This devotional to Frigg and Her handmaidens shares insights and experiences which I hope will further your own spiritual journey. Although they are worthy of all honor, I will not discuss goddesses such as such as Holda, Frau Holle, Perchta, or Berchta who are often linked in function. Although I will discuss and cite scholarly sources, this is, first and foremost, a work of the heart and spirit. The purpose of this devotional is not to master the lore and delve into scholarly sources, but to open ourselves to and make a connection with the divine. I have organized the headings in the devotional section around my calls to Frigg in a song of invocation I wrote for a blót that has been recorded on the Assembly of the Sacred Wheel's chant album, *Dreams Sung True*. I hope that this devotional to Frigg will help you to open yourself to Her and to feel the tenderness and power of that connection. I hope that this devotional will help you to draw closer to Frigg and to help you to become frith weavers in your communities.

Frigg as envisioned by Jenny Nyström, in Sander,
Edda Sämund den Vises (1893)

Chapter 1: Unverified Personal Gnosis (aka UPG)

Modern societies generally judge reality by what can be quantified, figured out with math and physics, and verified in some logical manner. *Gnosis* refers to knowledge based on personal experience or perception. In a religious context, gnosis is mystical or esoteric knowledge based on direct participation with the divine. Because it is personal in nature, and the interpretation is more a matter of the heart and spirit than the mundane, such gnosis need not be verified. If some folk have an issue with *unverified personal gnosis* (UPG), it is that it is unverifiable by definition. Although everyone is entitled to believe and be inspired by their personal experiences of deity, it is wise to compare your experiences with those of others and with the lore. If you are a member of a garth, kindred, stead, coven, or online group, you can compare experiences with other members and can discuss your experiences during vision, seidr, ritual, and dreams with them.

All of the stories that we have were once unverified personal gnosis that became substantiated personal gnosis through the shared experience of many people and over time, Of course, times change, and our practice must adapt, grow, and change as well, but the lore provides a basis for our beliefs. I have a healthy respect for unverified personal gnosis; in fact, I prefer to call it just personal gnosis. What you or I experience through meditation, visioning, ritual, and dreams is profound and sometimes life-changing, and the word "unverified" seems to diminish the importance of these experiences. It's fine if other people's personal gnosis contradicts mine, because it's private and personal—a matter of one's unique history, energy, emotions, and thoughts coloring the experience. Or a deity may come calling in an aspect that is meant just for you.

Of course, one single instance of experiencing Frigg wearing a light blue apron dress or Freyr riding a golden boar would be personal gnosis. But when thousands of folk over time perceive Thor's beard to be red, Odin's cape as grey/black/midnight blue, Frigg's colors to be blue and white and her energy as loving, organized, and practical—we then have substantiated gnosis that is often incorporated into our lore and customs. I believe that our ancestors, like the little völva (seeress) in *Erik the Red's Saga*, learned about the gods and goddesses through UPG much as we do today.

I have experienced Frigg and her handmaidens through aspecting (a form of drawing down or deity possession), images, dreams, symbols, songs, and conversations. Communication with our deities, landvaettir, house wights, alfar, disir, and other beings inspire and encourage our spiritual journeys. For me, Frigg is very straightforward and grounded. She is never flashy or dramatic, and her guidance is almost always quiet and firm; it isn't the psychic equivalent of being grabbed and shaken until your teeth rattle (which is the *modus operandi* of other deities I've aspected). She encourages order and tidiness. If you have asked Frigg to be a part of your life, her altar and statues or images of her should be dusted, and you should strive to keep your mundane affairs in order. If you ask and offer, she will guide and support your efforts. Frigg's quiet but insistent support helps me get on with my mundane and spiritual work as a frithweaver, as a witch and godwoman. In fact, she planted the seeds for this devotional in the year that I had bilateral mastectomies. Despite my doubts, she knew that I could do this, and through communication with her and support from others on this path, I have manifested what she inspired.

She is quiet, no-nonsense, and loving but firm. She understands and is honored by my small acts of love and devotion. Tidying an altar, mopping the floor, cleaning dishes, cooking a meal with love and good will are all ways of honoring the Lady of hearth and home. She has taught me that great relationships and connections are built from small acts of love and consideration. The choices we make to be weavers of frith, even in our smallest acts, are like seeds that grow into a beautiful orchard that bears sweet and nourishing fruit.

Chapter 2: Frigg in the Lore and Other Sources

.   My goal in this chapter is to provide a brief overview of Frigg as She appears in the Lore and other ancient sources which, I hope, will deepen your understanding as you engage with the devotions to Frigg and Her Handmaidens in later chapters. If you would like to pursue further academic study, I suggest the works of scholars such as H.R. Ellis Davidson, Ursula Dronke, Carolyne Larrington, Rudolf Simek, John Lindow, Jackson Crawford, and Jesse Byock, as well as the excellent works of Kveldulf Gundarsson, Diana Paxson, Patricia Lafayllve, Alice Karlsdóttir, and the volumes of *Our Troth*.

Frigg is an ancient goddess, whose lands of worship spanned Scandinavia, continental Germanic regions, and Anglo-Saxon Britain. *Frigg* (Old Norse) and *Frija* (Old High German) can be traced to the Proto-Indo-European noun **priya* or "one's own; dear, beloved one" (Gundarsson 2007). Frigg's name can be traced back to a people who lived from roughly 4500 to 2500 B.C. The term *frith*, active good will and dynamic peace within a group, also springs from this root. Her worship was so significant that Romans of the 3rd and 4th century CE equated Frigg to Venus, and their weekday, *dies Veneris*, was equivalent to the Old Norse *fríadagr* and Old English *frigedaeg*, or Friday (Simek and Hall 2007). They also associated Frigg (as well as Freyja) with Venus; the planet was called *friggjarstjarna*, "Frigg's star." *Friggjargras*, "Frigg's herb," was the name of an orchid that was used for love magic (Karlsdóttir 2015).

Just as Odin is the All-Father, Frigg is the All-Mother. In *Egil's Saga*, the poet Egill Skallagrimsson refers to the gods collectively as "Frigg's progeny" (Smiley 2005). As you will see, She is Odin's only "official" wife, but She does not show any animosity to his other partners. She is a seeress with foreknowledge who refrains from speaking of what she knows. Some scholars consider Her twelve handmaidens to be her *hypostases*, beings who flow forth from Her own being; but even if they are fully separate goddesses without this energetic connection, they are still a part of Her team—ministers in Her Cabinet so to speak. The term "handmaid" is in no way pejorative, as attendance on a queen is an honor, and each goddess fulfills important functions linked to Frigg's authority and energies.

Frigg engages and invests her time and energy in the mortal world and can even outwit Odin to gain Her objectives. She is a goddess of motherhood, hearth, home, frith and the domestic arts, but She is also the queen of Asgard and acts as counselor, tactician, protectress, giver of sovereignty, CEO, guide, spinner of wyrd, and healer. Chapter One of *Skáldskaparmál* says that She is one of the goddesses who sits on the council of judges, and She alone is permitted to sit with Odin on Hlidskjalf, the high seat that overlooks the Nine Worlds. Her abilities and powers span more than any one category. As She has a cart pulled by rams, and the Swedes called Orion's belt *Friggerock* (Frigg's spindle), She is connected to spinning, the mundane fiber arts, and the related activities of the spinning and weaving of wyrd.

Most scholars acknowledge that it is nigh impossible to date the point of origin of myths that surface in later written texts. Although thirteenth-century mythological texts do reflect the earlier mythology, this uncertainty makes it hard to determine how much actual pagan content still exists in mythological texts from the medieval period. Heathenry has been called "the religion with homework" for good reason, and any practicing Heathen, or anyone following a Northern Tradition practice, should validate their practice at least in part through a knowledge of historical and archeological evidence and by reading the primary sources provided in the lore. Most folk are not rock-bound fundamentalists; rather, we acknowledge that we can be grateful for the records we have from the medieval period and before, and base our contemporary practices on the lore, substantiated personal gnosis (what many folk have experienced throughout heathenry and generationally as recorded in the lore and folk tradition), and through our personal encounters with the divine (UPG or unverified personal gnosis).

Frigg in the Eddas

Modern Heathens base their beliefs and practices in part upon the Elder Edda, a.k.a. the *Poetic Edda*. A compilation of thirty-nine poems composed by a variety of anonymous Icelandic authors, the *Poetic Edda* gives us insight into the spiritual practices and heroic ethics of pre-Christian Scandinavian and Germanic cultures. Discovered in the *Codex Regius*, the Royal Book, these poems are believed to have been composed between 800–1100 CE. The original poets, known as skalds, did not have a tradition of written documents; the written documents date from the post-conversion period (1050-1350 CE).

In chapter 35 of the *Prose Edda*'s *Gylfaginning*, Snorri states that Frigg's hall is Fensalir (Marsh Hall), and that She is the foremost of the goddesses. In Snorri's *Skáldskaparmál* (Poetic Diction), he states that Frigg should be referred to as "the daughter of Fjörgynn, the wife of Odin, the mother of Baldr (killed by Hod), the rival paramour of Earth, Rind, Gunnlod and Gerd, the mother in law of Nanna, or the queen of the gods and goddesses, of Fulla, of the falcon's feather cloak and of the halls of Fensalir" (Byock 2005). Although she is the foremost Ásynja of the tribe of the Æsir, her father, Fjörgynn, may have been Jotun ("giant"), and it is speculated that he may have been the partner of Fjörgyn which is another name for Jordh—a jotun who personifies the Earth itself.

Frigg's cult may have become hidden or eclipsed by Christian beliefs by the time these poems were recorded. Still, as John Lindow points out, Frigg's name appears in many Scandinavian place-names "indicating cult activity" (Lindow 2002, p. 129). Frigg's importance as cited in the Eddas and other sources, makes it clear that She was widely honored in Germanic culture, and that Her many roles are important to both gods and humans. The lore emphasizes her power and importance to the clan of the Æsir and Ásynjur and to mortals dwelling in Midgard.

Frigg is first mentioned in stanzas 34 and 51[1] of the *Poetic Edda*'s *Völuspá*, the prophesy of the seeress. The passages tell of Frigg's grief upon the death of her son, Baldr at the hands of his half-brother Hod at the instigation of Loki, "And in Fen-halls Frigg wept / for Valhall's woe" (*Seeress's Prophecy*, 34) These stanzas depict Frigg as grieving mother and wife. But she, as the All-Mother, goddess of foreknowledge and frith weaver, also grieves for "Valhall's woe"—the grief of her tribe, who will all suffer from Baldr's death, and the wyrd spun, the choices that will be made as a result of this tragedy. We learn that her hall, Fensalir, is in the fens/

---

1. Please note that I use Carolyne Larrington's translation. As the original document's stanzas were unnumbered, different translations number them with slight differences. If you have a different translation, the quoted stanza may have a different numeral, but should be in the ballpark. Also, the translators' word choice may differ, and unless you speak Old Norse, consider reading more than one translation to gain a fuller understanding of the verse.

marshes. Like the Germanic mother goddess deity, Nerthus, this attaches her to liminal places, both earth and water.

> Then *Frigg's* [ON *Hlínar*] second sorrow [ON *annarr*] comes about
> When Odin advances to fight the wolf,
> And Beli's bright slayer [*Freyr*] against Surt;
> Then Frigg's dear beloved [literally sweet scent, ON *angan*] must fall.
> (*Seeress's Prophecy* V.51)

Many modern scholars and translators interpret the phrase *Friggjar angan*, Frigg's beloved/joy, as Odin. In verse 54, either as a kenning or as a direct association, Frigg is equated with Hlín, one of Frigg's attendants or hypostases. The Old Norse word *hlína* means to hide or protect, which links Frigg to the role of protectress. There is a saying that one who escapes danger "leans" or finds refuge, *hlínar* (Karlsdóttir, 2015, p. 176). In the section on Her handmaidens we will focus on how she shares and delegates this function with the goddess Hlín. Frigg here is also a grieving wife who, for all her power and foresight, attempts to ward, guide, and turn wyrd, can no more prevent her husband's death than She could that of her son. Here we are twice shown that even the Great Ones lay down ørlög and are subject to wyrd.

Frigg next appears in *Vafþrúðnismál*, Vafthrudnir's Sayings, as both wise counselor and loving spouse. As in *Vǫluspá*, Odin quests for wisdom and especially for information about Ragnarok. Here we see Frigg in the role of counselor, as well as wife and queen concerned for Odin's safety both as husband as and ruler of Asgard. She bestows her blessings, both as wife and gythia.

> Odin said:
> 'Advise me, Frigg, for I long to journey
> To visit Vafthruthnir
> I've a great curiosity to contend in ancient matters
> With that all-wise giant.'

After Odin approaches Frigg and asks for her advice, Frigg replies by giving her counsel:

Frigg said:
'I'd rather keep the Father of Hosts
at home in the courts of the gods,
For I know no giant to be as powerful
As Vafthruthnir is.'

Her advice and her concern may suggest that She actually may not be in possession of foreknowledge of the fate of the Æsir when it involves the Jotuns, because, if she did know all that was fated to be, she would be aware that Odin's journey is no threat to him and that he will return victorious. In this instance she does not encourage Odin's journey to Vafthruthnir, as she might if she knew that he would return. Unlike the seeress in *Völuspá*, Frigg was not aware (at that time) that Odin's death will occur at Ragnarök, which underscores the possibility that her foreknowledge does not extend into the word of the Jotuns and that Her foreknowledge has more to do with the wyrd of god/desses and humans and doesn't include the wyrd of Jotnar or a Jotun-affiliated god like Loki. In the case of Loki, it's a blind spot with tragic consequences.

Odin said:
'Much I have traveled, much have I tried out,
Much have I tested the Powers,
This I want to know; what kind of company
Is found in Vafthruthnir's hall.'

Frigg said:
'Journey safely! Come back safely!
Be safe on the way!
May your mind be sufficient when, Father of Men,
You speak with the giant.'

She was worried and concerned for her husband's safety, because from what she knows of Vafthruthnir, his intellect may be a match for Odin's. But Frigg knows that it is his nature to wander and quest for wisdom; instead of clinging to him, she bestows her blessings and protection on his journey.

Frigg as Strategist and Tactician

Like her husband, Frigg possesses the foresight, wit, wisdom, and political savvy necessary to rule Asgard and to influence human affairs. Frigg and Odin are twice portrayed as opponents. In the *Historia Langobardorum* (*History of the Langobards*), written in the 8th century, Odin supports the Vandals while Frigg supports the Vinils—renamed the Langobards by Odin, thanks to Frigg's cunning.

> The Vandals approached Wodan, beseeching from him victory over the Vinils. The god answered: "I will grant victory to the first ones I see at sunrise."
>
> Gambara, on the other hand, approached Frea, Wodan's wife, and beseeched from her victory for the Vinils. Frea responded with the advice that the Vinil women should untie their hair and arrange it across their face like a beard, and that they should thus accompany their men in the early morning to the window from which Wodan customarily looked out.
>
> They did as they were advised, and at sunrise, Wodan, upon looking out, shouted: "Who are these Longbeards?"
>
> Frea replied: "To the ones you give a name, you must also give victory." And thus Wodan gave them the victory, and from that time forth the Vinils have been called Longbeards [Langobards]. (Foulke translation, 1974, ch. 8)

Frigg's formidable skills as a strategist and tactician are also relayed in the *Poetic Edda*'s *Grímnismál*, where Frigg and Odin are the rival patrons and foster parents of two princes. What is very clear is that Frigg takes a manifest interest in human affairs and (as she fosters a different child from Odin) has her own agenda. As in *Historia Langobardorum*, Frigg proves herself to be Odin's equal as She develops and implements a plan of action. So, Odin, who disguised as a farmer, fosters Geirrod and Frigg, as the farmer's wife, fosters Agnar. To some extent, the children are pawns in their rivalry, and although they care for their foster sons, their tactics towards their opposition, mortal and immortal, are no-holds-barred. It's always a good idea to remember that the gods and goddesses have their own agendas, and your part may not be the one you expected. Odin strikes first and has his foster son abandon and curse his brother—which is the type of consequentialist ethical choice (in which his foster son receives the greatest good) that one would expect from the All Father.

> In the springtime, the farmer got them a boat. When he and his wife were leading them down to the beach, the farmer said something to Geirrod alone. They had a fair wind, and came into their father's harbor. Geirrod was forward in the boat; he leaped out on shore, thrust the ship back, and shouted "Get out, and may the trolls take you!" The boat sailed away, and Geirrod went up toward the houses and was warmly welcomed. His father had died in the meantime. Geirrod became king and won great fame. (Larrington 2014, p. 48)

The next scene demonstrates the equality of Odin and Frigg, as they both sit upon Hlidskjalf—a high seat (a supernatural platform, so to speak) from which only Odin and Frigg are permitted to view the nine worlds. The fact that Frigg and only Frigg is permitted this privilege (although Freyr uses it without permission in *Skírnismál*) emphasizes her rank and status. There is a sense of one-upmanship here, as well as a sense of propriety over their respective charges.

> One day Odin and Frigg were sitting in Hlidskjalf looking out over all the worlds. Odin said, "Do you see your foster-son Agnar begetting children with a giantess in a cave? But Geirrod, my foster son, is a king and rules the land." Frigg said: "He is so stingy with food that he tortures his guests if it seems to him too many have come" (Larrington, 2014, p. 48).

Frigg's observation is a great insult, as such lack of hospitality, especially in a king, would be a great infraction against the custom of hospitality and the duty owed to a guest by his host. Odin denies Frigg's accusation, and the no-holds-barred-wager is on. Just as wily Odin whispered an underhanded tactic to Geirrod, Frigg has Fulla, a goddess of hidden wisdom who shares Frigg's secrets, set a different set of wheels in motion. Since Frigg has foreknowledge of god/desses and humans, she must know that Odin will suffer for the betrayal of her own foster son, but will not ultimately be harmed. She also knows that Odin's foster son Geirrod, who betrayed and cursed his own brother, will die. Then frith and justice will be served when a compassionate king (Agnar the Second), made wise from Odin's teachings, will reign. Thus Frigg, the first-rate strategist, avenges Odin and Geirrod's betrayal of her own foster son, Agnar, when Odin causes Geirrod to fall on his own sword.

> Frigg sent her handmaid, Fulla, to Geirrod. She told the king to beware lest a wizard, who had come into the country, should bewitch him, and said he could be known by this sign: the fact that no dog, no matter how savage, would attack him. And that was the greatest slander that Geirrod was not generous with food. But he had the man arrested whom no dog would attack. He was wearing a blue cloak and called himself Grimnir and would say nothing more about himself, though he was asked. The king had him tortured to make him speak and set him between two fires; and he sat there for eight nights. . . King Geirrod sat with a sword in his lap half-drawn from the sheath. When he heard that his visitor was Odin, he stood up, intending to take Odin away from the fires. The sword slipped out of his hand and fell, hilt down. The king stumbled and fell forward against the point of the sword; and so he died. Odin vanished. Then Agnar was king in that land for a long time. (Larrington 2014, pp. 48, 56)

Frigg in *Lokasenna*, Loki's Quarrel

In the Poetic Edda's *Lokasenna*, "Loki's Quarrel," Frigg, Odin, and all of the Æsir and Ásynjur are assembled for a feast in Aegir's hall. Loki crashes the party and proceeds to insult everyone (except Thor). Loki and Odin exchange insults, and Frigg steps in to caution them without, it should be noted, denying their charges and countercharges:

> 'The fates you met should never be
> told in front of people,
> what you two Æsir underwent in past times;
> the living should keep their distance from ancient matters.
> (Larrington 2014, p. 48; verse 25)

Frigg here cautions them to be circumspect about their past deeds and the orlog they laid through those choices. Frigg interceeds in her role as frithweaver. Instead of insulting Loki and instigating more strife, she cautions. Instead of focusing on Loki's Jotun blood, she names him Æsir through his blood-brotherhood with Odin and his own identification as Laufeysson—assuming that Laufey was a member of the ásynjur. Despite Frigg's best efforts, Loki, whose aim here is unfrith, goads her:

> Loki said:
> 'Be silent Frigg, you're Fjörgyn's daughter [ON *Fjörgyns mær*]
> And you've always been man-mad:
> Ve and Vili, Vidrir's [Odin's] wife,
> You took them both in your embrace.
> (Larrington 2014, p. 85; verse 26)

In verse 26 Loki call Frigg, Fjörgynn's *mær*, which is usually translated as daughter or maid. So Fjörgynn is Frigg's parent. Unfortunately, the 12th and 13th century recordings of this name are problematic as the name shifts form male to female form depending upon scholarly interpretation. In *Skaldskaparmal* 19, Snorri also identifies Frigg as the daughter of Fjörgyn or Jörð. The name Fjörgyn appears in Skaldic poetry at times as a synonym for "earth" or "land" (Lindow 2002, p. 117). In its feminine form, Fjörgyn is Jord the earth, and Thor's mother. This would make Frigg both Thor's half-sister and his stepmother! However, some scholars identify this parent as Fjörgynn—the male form of the name. Rudolf Simek identifies Fjörgynn as Frigg's father; "it seems more likely that Fjörgynn is a late analogous formation to Fjörgyn, but there have been attempts to link with the [thunder] god Perkunas" (Simek 2007, p. 86).

Therefore, a number of scholarly theories surround the names, and it seems that different translators will use one over the other when translating the same verse. The feminine form, "Fjörgyn," is recorded in stanza 56 of the Poetic Edda's *Hárbarðsljóð*, but I have read translations that use masculine forms. Chapter 9 of the Prose Edda's *Gylfaginning* states: "His wife was called Frigg, Fjörgyn's daughter, and from this family has come the kindred we call the family of the Æsir" (Byock 2005.18). Hilda Ellis Davidson theorizes that like Ullr and Ullin, Njörðr and Nerthus, and Freyr and Freyja, Fjörgyn and Fjörgynn may have represented a divine pair (Davidson 1969, p. 106). Alice Karlsdóttir states that, while Jord (ON "earth") is the primal, undomesticated earth, Frigg is the fruitful tilled earth, "that has been transformed by her alliance with humans" (Karlsdóttir 2015, p. 52). My own work with Frigg inclines me towards Davidson's theory, that at least one and possibly both of Frigg's parents were members of a divine pair—powerful beings linked to the Earth and possibly to sky energies. This does not make Frigg any less an Ásynja, as even Odin is descended from Jotun stock through his mother, Bestla. What we can glean from the lore is that Frigg is connected to the energies of the earth through her parentage, and through the watery, liminal realm of marshland, through her hall Fensalir, and possibly to a cult of springs associated with Her (Simek 2007, p. 81)

Loki's accusation of Frigg's infidelity also appears in *Ynglinga Saga* 3, when Odin's brothers Vili and Vé share Frigg until Odin's return. Saxo Grammaticus' version of Odin's exile also asserts that She was unfaithful to Odin. How much of this material has been affected by Christian morality is unknown, but we can see even in the lore that exists that Odin isn't overly distressed by the accusation, and certainly Frigg never complained about Odin's many liaisons. Several scholars theorize that this account of Odin's wandering and his brothers acting in His stead is connected to an older story and that, as the queen of Asgard, it was Frigg's duty to bestow and maintain the sovereignty in her husband's absence. As Vili and Vé stand in for Odin and are often considered his hypostases, it makes sense that she would maintain Asgard's functionality by fulfilling her role as consort.

In verse 27, we see that Frigg is fiercely devoted to her only son Baldr, whom she knows will defend her against Loki's taunts.

> Frigg said:
> You know that if I had here in Aegir's hall
> a boy like my Baldr,
> you wouldn't get away from the Æsir's sons;
> they'd be furious fighting against you.
> (Larrington 2014, p. 85; verse 27)

In verse 28 Loki asserts his role in Baldr's death which he himself calls wicked:

> Loki said:
> Frigg, you want me to say more about
> my wicked deeds
> for I brought it about that you will never again
> see Baldr ride to the halls.
> (Larrington 2014, p. 85; verse 28)

It seems that Loki wants to make Frigg feel this grief and animosity even more keenly. One wonders what motivates such spite, as it will inevitably bring about more suffering for both himself and the Æsir.

At this point Frigg becomes silent, and the goddess Freyja warns Loki:

> Mad are you, Loki, when you reckon up your
> Ugly, hateful deeds;
> Frigg knows, I think, all fate,
> Though she herself does not speak out.
> (Larrington 2014, p. 85, verse 29)

What Frigg Knows

I have discussed the fact that there is some confusion in the lore regarding how much Frigg knows. As I discussed earlier, it seems that she has all, or at least vast, knowledge of the wyrd of God/desses and mortals, but seems to have a blind spot when the Jotnar are concerned. She doesn't recognize Loki and tragically shares information about the mistletoe, and she is worried that Odin may not return from his journey to Vafthruthnir. Odin goes to the seeress, not to Frigg, for information about Ragnarok. *Völuspá's* seeress says that although Frigg has "much wisdom," it is not infinite that the seeress can "see further ahead" (Larrington 2014, verse 43).

It's hard to believe that Odin could not have sought information closer to home if Frigg could supply it. Yet Freya, a great seeress and witch in her own right, says that she thinks Frigg knows "all fate." This knowledge of fate and her association with birth connects Frigg to the Nornir, the principal weavers of fate and destiny. Despite what Freyja asserts, it becomes obvious in the *Prose Edda*'s *Baldrs Draumr* that Frigg's knowledge, at least when it comes to the motives of beings who are neither mortal nor Æsir, may indeed be limited.

It is also worth noting that she "does not speak out" about her knowledge, but she most certainly acts upon her knowledge, as we see in *Baldrs Draumr*. Some scholars feel that Frigg's reticence to speak out comes from a sense that not speaking about what she knows might somehow delay the inevitable and keep the events from becoming more immediate.

Frigg and Baldr's Death

The *Prose Edda*'s descriptions of Baldr's death provide more insight into Frigg's personality and especially into her role as Asgard's mother goddess—willing to move forces across the realms to rectify the catastrophe. Baldr, the son of Odin and Frigg, has a series of dreams foreboding his death. The gods hold council and decide to seek a truce with all harmful things to protect Baldr from harm. Frigg is the instigator and active participant who presides over oaths from fire, water, iron, all objects, animals, and birds, snakes, poisons, and diseases that they will not harm Baldr. Frigg's role in administering and hearing these oaths is a mark of her role as Baldr's mother, Queen of Asgard and as a member of the god/desses' council.

As I will discuss in the section on Var, from ancient times to current, an oath is a potent, binding promise heard across the worlds for Heathens. Frigg's power and authority is so great that these wights remain true to their oaths. Only the mistletoe seemed too young to her, and so she did not require its oath. This particular passage, as well as the Volva's statement in *Völuspá*, indicates that while Frigg may know the fates of gods and men, she seems unable to foresee the activities of Loki or the giants; only a volva like the seeress knows these things, which is why Odin ventures beyond the counsel of his prescient wife, and journeys to consult the seeresses in *Völuspá* and *Baldrs draumar*. Furthermore, for all of her wisdom, Frigg cannot foresee Loki's designs or even his disguise as a woman when s/he seeks Frigg out at Fensalir: "Then Frigg said, 'Neither weapons nor wood will harm Baldr. I have received oaths from all of them.'" Loki asks whether all things have given their oaths to Frigg. Frigg confides that she hasn't required the young mistletoe to swear an oath and does not perceive what *Völuspá*'s Seeress so clearly does—that the mistletoe would become "a dangerous grief-dart" that would end Baldr's life (Larrington 2014, *Völuspá*, verse 33). Loki hastens to procure the mistletoe, gives it to the blind god Hod, and makes sure that Hod's aim is true and Baldr falls to the ground dead.

Frigg's astonishing lack of foresight gives Loki the knowledge he needs to murder Baldr and she is wracked (as any parent would be) with extreme grief, fury, and guilt. Frigg attends her son's and daughter-in-law's cremation, and it is at her request that Odin's son Hermod rides to Hel to petition for Baldr's return. Hel grants this on the condition that all things weep for him. Loki, disguised as the giantess Thokk ("Gratitude," ironically enough), refuses to weep and proclaims, "Let Hel hold what she has" (Byock 2005, p. 69). Loki and his malicious Jotun nature is a force even Frigg did not foresee as a threat. There is a terrible irony in the fact that Frigg, in all her wisdom, discounted the power of the seemingly weak and utterly harmless mistletoe in the hands of expert malice. In a later meditation we will ponder what we can all learn from this tragedy.

Frigg and Healing in the Lore

Frigg is noted as a healer and a protector of women. In the *Poetic Edda*'s *Oddrúnargrátr*, "Oddrún's Lament," Borgny, the daughter of King Heidrek, is having problems during childbirth and Atli's sister, Oddrún, sang "sharp spells (*galdr*) for Borgny" (Larrington 2014, p. 200, verse 7). When Oddrun's *galdr* is successful and Borgny gives birth to twins, she blesses Oddrún: "May the kindly beings help you / Frigg and Freyja and more of the gods / as you warded off that dangerous illness from me" (Larrington 2014, p. 200) In "The Second Merseburg Charm," Frigg is among the goddesses who lend their healing skills to cure Balder's horse of lameness:

> There Balder's foal
> sprained its foot. . .
> It was charmed by Frija,
> her sister Volla
> (Ashliman 1998)

Frigg also selected Eir, the goddess of healing and "best of doctors." to be available for all folk in need of healing, and she is part of Frigg's court and an extension of Frigg's purview and power.

Frigg as envisioned by Johannes Gehrts,
redrawn for Guerber, *Myths of Northern Lands* (1895)

Chapter 3: Devotions

This chapter expresses my thoughts and perceptions of Frigg in some of her many roles. I have organized the heading according to the praise names that I use for her in a song of invocation I wrote for a blót that you will find in the chapter of songs and poems to Frigg and her handmaidens. The invocation to Frigg is recorded on the Assembly of the Sacred Wheel's wonderful chant album *Dreams Sung True*, and can also be found on YouTube. I hope that this method of organization will draw you closer to Frigg and that, after reading this chapter, the praise names in the song will have a deeper meaning for you.

Frigg—All Mother

> *Being a mother is an attitude, not a biological relation.*
> —Robert A. Heinlein

Frigg is the fierce and loving biological mother of Baldr, but She is also the foster parent of the human prince Agnar, and the stepmother to Odin's children by other mothers. She is also a mother to all who are devoted to Her. She will always inspire us to create a foundation of trust on which to build frith and a loving relationship. If you are a stepparent, legal guardian or a foster parent, Frigg is there to guide and support you.

All Mother
Who fostered Agnar with love
Mother of Baldr,
Stepmother of Víðarr, Váli, Thor, Hermóðr and all of Odin's children
Give me perseverance even when I feel rejected
Give me the strength and courage
to build a foundation of trust and respect.
Help me to be honest and authentic
and to reach out with love
Even when I don't feel like it

Open my eyes to special moments and
Unexpected gifts.
—Maire Durkan

To describe my mother would be to write about a hurricane in its perfect
power. Or the climbing, falling colors of a rainbow.
—Maya Angelou

Maya Angelou's quote describes the great power of motherhood. It is the power of conception, birth, mothering in all its myriad aspects. It is the power and conviction of unconditional love and the manifestation of that love in a lifetime of acts of love both great and small. This is Motherhood with a capital "M." But in the mundane word, motherhood is a paradox where happiness, jobs well done, wonder and triumphant milestones contend with frustrations, quarrels, obstacles, and just plain mess. As both the hands-on mother attending to her family and the All-Mother, Frigg understand this paradox and we can call on her to help us find a balance.

One of the ways that I relate to Frigg as the Great Mother is through the runic energy of Berkano (ᛒ), the great goddess rune of growth, protection, rebirth and renewal. It has always been Frigg's rune for me. Birch has many medicinal and magical properties including warding and protection, instilling courage and healing. Berkano has the energy of a birch grove, and is a sanctuary in times of need. The birch is the first tree to awaken in the spring time, and so Berkano is about the cycle of birth, death and rebirth.

> *Hail Frigg!*
> *May the energy of Berkano flow through me*
> *May my personal creativity flow*
> *May the works I manifest be genuine and true*
> *To my personal walk and vision*
> *May I be firmly rooted in the world and connected to the*
> *Nurturing energy of the Earth*
> *Yet, like the slender birch, be flexible and strong enough*
> *To withstand the storms, I will encounter*
> *To bend without breaking*

And always find sanctuary
In your energy of regeneration and renewal
—Maire Durkan

The phrase 'working mother' is redundant.
—Jane Sellman

Mothering is a verb—a way of being that transcends biology and relates just as much to adopted and foster children. Ultimately, a loving bond is woven from physical and emotional care and nurturing the parent gives a child. As the child grows the gifts given will be reciprocated in all manner of ways. Sometimes the "gift" may come through trials—the gift of patience received when raising your tween or teen for instance! And all parents have had to contend with heartache and the realization that our children are their own people and must stumble and make mistakes that we cannot right. Our desire to save our child or children and make their world our version of right is one of our most powerful instincts. Sometimes our choice to step in is justified and sometimes we need to step back and let our children learn and accept the consequences of their choices. Frigg understands this all too well and she will support us through hard choices and tough love.

That being said, starting with their first kicks and through all the years of our lives together and apart, each of my children and I formed a bond that is nigh on unbreakable—even by distance, trials, and tribulations. My oldest children are now in their mid-thirties and although they've gone their own ways and formed new relationships and bonds, the bond we share is still there.

From the apple flushed down the toilet and the salami cast with glee upon the ceiling where it leaves an indelible greasy ring, to teenage bumper thumpers and break-ups, we learn that our children are going to get hurt, make mistakes and, hopefully, learn and grow because of those experiences. Not a day go by when I do not pray that the ancestors and the Great Ones protect them. But there's a line between going to bat for a child when they truly require your aid and hovering/smothering and crippling their ability make their own choices and problem solve for themselves. Frigg is a fierce and loving mother and the patroness and guardian

19

to all parents—biological, foster, or step. She's there to support you when you need her the most, but she will also give you the space to make choices, make mistakes, and learn from them.

As Odin has many children by other partners, Frigg has many stepsons (Thor being among them)—and probably stepdaughters. Both in the lore (see how she fosters Agnar) and in my personal experience, Frigg makes it clear that mothering is not smothering, and that parents who overprotect and bend over backwards to make sure their kids succeed are actually not giving them the space they need to try and to make decisions for themselves. In the days before our youngest teenage sons flew off to a remote organic farm in the mountains of Idaho, I lay awake until the wee hours worrying about all the aspects of these six weeks that were out of my control (what if they got sick, what if they got lost, what if...) So, in my turmoil, I turned to Frigg All Mother and had a heart-to-heart.

Frigg said, "What if you held on to them so tightly that your grip became a tether that crippled them? It's time to let go for a little while, so that you can let go and they can walk away with confidence later. So, they'll get lost [they did on back roads while biking] and then they'll find their way [they did after many hours] and they'll be proud because the figured it out for themselves [they were]."

She remined me that we must remember our own triumphs and that some of the proudest, most confidence boosting memories we have are of things that we accomplished by ourselves. Like Frigg with Agnar (she didn't swoop in, hit Geirrod upside the head, and bring the boat ashore), we need to give our children the chance to succeed or fail, on their own merit because we love them so deeply.

Let's do a quick word association. Without peeking at mine, think of words that you associate with "mother."

Thinking of my own mother, mine would be loving, nurturing, compassionate, supportive, patient, courageous, wise and irreplaceable. I hope that all of you can, at least find some good words to associate with you mother or with a guardian who fulfilled that roll for you. I hope that you can and will find words that apply to your parenting that make you proud and that you recognize those traits to which you aspire.

Care for The Caregiver

As the All Mother—not just of the gods and goddesses but of human-kind and especially of those who follow a Heathen or Northern Tradition path, we are all Frigg's children and we are all connected to her. Like all mothers, her hope for us is that we become individuals who are strong and whole spiritually, emotionally and physically, whose lives have more joy and love than burdens, and who contribute to and have positive connec-tions and support with their families and communities. She aches with a mother's compassion when life breaks and bends us—when we feel hurt beyond healing and aren't sure what our next step can be or dread the step that we must take. Parents tend to burn out—there are so many demands and responsibilities! But before we can take care of others, we must take care of ourselves. I learned the hard way that I am no use to my family if I have not taken care of my own needs.

Frigg would say to you as she has said to me, "Dear one, you are more than your age, your weight, your health, your income, your roles. You are my beloved child, doing the work you were put on Midgard to do in this time and place. You must nurture yourself to know yourself. You are more than the sum of your connections and responsibilities. Do not let them define you for they are only a small part of who you truly are! We are connected and my love and power are connected to your own ability to nurture, encourage, care for, act and speak with compassion. But first, dearest, you must have compassion for yourself."

Prayer for Self Nurturing

All Mother—Mother of All
You tell me "You too are beloved."
Help me to love and care for myself
So that I can truly love and care for others
May I see myself clearly, both light and dark,
And learn and evolve in a healthy way
Knowing and accepting who I am
Embracing my strengths and acknowledging and working on my weak-
*   nesses*

May I have the courage to look honestly
And remove those things from my life
That do not serve my progress,
May I regard myself with compassion
May I see the beauty in who I am
May I know that I am worthy of love
And move forward in this life
So that I may be a support and comfort to others.
—Maire Durkan

Self-acceptance meditation:

Visualize yourself glazing into a clear pool of water. Look into your eyes and acknowledge the emotions and feelings that you have in this moment. Now beside your image visualize the All Mother standing next to you. She holds out her hand and you take it. Look into her eyes. Know her unconditional love for you, her child of spirit.

As her love and compassion touches every fiber of your being, say, "I am loved. I am worthy of love."

When you rise in the morning, ask Frigg to help you manifest caring and nurturing today.

Queen

"Leaders instill in their people a hope for success and a belief in themselves. Positive leaders empower people to accomplish their goals."
—Unknown

My oldest daughter and I visited a local museum of decorative arts to view costumes from a dramatized history of the reign of Queen Elizabeth II. Although exquisite, the queen's coronation robes, gown, gloves, orb, scepter and crown were not meant to be comfortable. Each elaborate appliqued and embroidered image was symbolic of some aspect of queenship, governance, and her kingdom. As part of the ceremony of coronation, the queen swears oaths, is anointed, is invested with garments, and is hailed as queen. During this powerful rite a woman takes on the office of queen as a living symbol of her people and an embodiment of her nation's identity.

There is a difference between the private individual and her public office as much for Frigg as for a mortal monarch. When Frigg became Odin's wife, her identity transitioned from being Fjörgyn's maid to being the Queen of Asgard. Like a mortal queen, her identity took on a new dimension. As Queen, Frigg is the focus for her people's identity, unity and pride. She gives the inhabitants of Asgard and all of those who follow a Northern tradition path a sense of continuity. In her capacity as queen, she embodies, power, legitimacy, honor, stability, and glory.

She sits on the counsel of the god/desses, shares the Hlidskjálf with Odin, strategizes, and organizes. She grants audiences, recognizes excellence, advises, hears oaths, awards favor, appoints and delegates, and acts as a royal patroness to those who follow her path. If you call upon Frigg in her aspect of queen, you call upon her functions as the head of state and the queen of Asgard and Midgard who is the quintessence of our spiritual path. Her handmaidens, especially Var who also witnesses oaths and punishes oath breakers and Fulla who shares her secrets and holds counsel with her, assist her in this role.

We can also call upon Frigg as Queen to help us balance our public and private lives. In modern times, Frigg, who has been compared to a CEO, still delegates specific functions to her handmaidens. She understands that the part of our self attached to our job, volunteer work, or a hobby, is not who we are (or not for me at least), when we come home and kick off our shoes. When I lead a blót in my capacity as a Troth gythia in my official role as godperson, my energies are focused on the rite, the holy beings, and the participants for whom I am performing my function as gythia; I'm not acting as a mom who drives my daughter to the doctor's office or cooks dinner. Although I relate to Frigg more fully in other aspects of her being, I cannot ignore her queenship and invoke her aid in representing Heathen values as a Heathen godwoman. I ask her aid in knowing which of Her handmaidens, I should work with in different situations, and how to do my best as a godperson. When I call upon her as the Queen of Asgard, I approach her with a sense of awe for she represents our way of life and our spiritual path. What she bestows, we incorporate into our spiritual and mundane lives.

Hail Frigg
Queen of Asgard,
First among the Ásynjur,
Queen of Strategy and Forethought,
Queen of the Folk!
Wise Counselor,
grant me the wisdom to discern my roles and responsibilities,
To efficiently utilize my abilities
and to reach out to those who have resources that I lack.
Instill in me the perseverance
to fulfill my responsibilities with honor
standing by any oath I take.
Help me to persevere until my tasks are complete,
find joy in a job well done
and learn through my failures and victories.
Help me to work frithfully and honorably with others.
May I lead with empathy, integrity, commitment, and creativity.
As you delegate work to your Handmaidens,
who reflect your vision,
May I delegate work to those who can best accomplish the task
and may I value and work for the empowerment of my innangarths!
—Maire Durkan

Further activities:

- Make a list of your roles.
- How do you fulfill them?
- In what ways is this role separate from your personal life?
- In what way does it reflect some aspect of your personality?

Beloved

Love is or it ain't. Thin love ain't love at all.
— Toni Morrison, *Beloved*

Falling in love is just that—we're over the moon, out of control, free falling! When we fall in love, we feel an immediate powerful attraction. If you've "got it bad," you long to be with the object of your affection all day every day. But if the relationship is going to become a long-term love relationship, falling in love must never become a "I'm sticking to you 'cause I'm made out of glue" codependency. Loving someone means you want to grow together and share common goals while supporting and encouraging your beloved's personal growth while attending to your own.

The lore demonstrates that Odin and Frigg share a loving, relationship composed of affection, camaraderie, and the ability to work together as a team toward common goals. Clearly, as is the case with the Lombards or in the case of their foster children, there is rivalry, but it never supersedes their love and respect for one another. And, if Odin is the bird (a bird of prey no doubt) in their relationship, Frigg is the hand (a well gloved hand like the hand of a falconer!).

Let's extend this metaphor. Frigg and Odin have been together for time immemorial. *Völuspá*'s seeress calls Odin Frigg's *angan*, her sweet scent—her beloved. They share the high seat together; they complement each other's functions, and it's obvious that they love and have great trust in the foundations of their relationship. Odin esteems her above all others, shares his seat, his rulership and secrets with her, and seeks her counsel. Frigg's is the hand from which Odin launches and flies free on his quests for knowledge and wisdom. Frigg and Odin "get" each other; she understands Odin and knows that he will always return to her. She realizes that if she clutches him too tightly, he might fly away forever. As she does in *Vafþrúðnismál*, she shares her concerns, but blesses his journey and return, "Journey safely! Come back safely! Be safe on the way!" (Larrington, 2014, p. 37). Their love has a firm foundation, built of a long loving relationship, built over countless years. They care for and support each other without stifling each other's independence—a perfect Venn diagram of a complex, functional, loving marriage, and one that we can all look to for inspiration.

Odin and Frigg as envisioned by Jurgen Moe (1875).
Courtesy of the National Library of Copenhagen

We do not often say, "This is my beloved friend / partner / *fulltrúa* / *fulltrúi*." But in our hearts we understand what the term "beloved" means to us. The one thing that all sentient beings share is a need to love and be loved and we all yearn not simply to love but to be someone's beloved. Remember that the root of Frigg's name is "beloved" and that she has earned that title through her care and nurturing for all of her children, immortal and mortal. You can turn to her and to her handmaidens, Sjofn and Lofn, for guidance in matters of the heart.

> *Dearest Wanderer*
> *My heart's angan,*
> *Sit by me while I spin the threads of wyrd.*
> *You are my heart's desire*
> *As I am yours.*
> *Long is it since I was that merry lass, Fjörgynn's maid,*
> *And yet I still desire you*
> *As you desire me*
> *Oski, embrace your beloved*
> *We will bring each other to ecstasy*
> *Beyond words and wisdom*
> *That is my gift to you.*

Afterwards, tell me of your travels
Of your hopes, fears, and dreams,
Let us laugh together
Before I must bless and ward your way once more.
　　　　　—Maire Durkan

Frigg and Open, Polyamorous, and Non-Binary Relationships

We can tell a lot about a person from their friends and associates or in Frigg's case, handmaidens. Two of Frigg's handmaidens, her delegates or hypostasis are Lofn (goddess of forbidden love—any love that is forbidden by family, clan, or community) and Sjofn (goddess of affection who turns the heart towards love). We know from the lore that Frigg and Odin enjoyed what we now call an open relationship. Frigg knows of Odin's other relationships and seems quite accepting and secure in her own place in Odin's heart. As she was accused by Loki, and does not deny, that she slept with his brothers when he was away for an extended time, I assume that the relationship was mutually open, but that Frigg only pursued other partners when the sovereignty of the realm made it necessary. As such, Frigg can be viewed as a patroness of loving relationships in which the partners have agreed to be open or polyamorous.

Most Beloved Lady,
May I find my beloved or beloveds
May our hearts' flames dance!
Open my heart to the bounty of loving relationships
Help me find the courage and insight to take this chance.
　　　　　—Maire Durkan

Frigg as Beloved Friend and Fully Trusted One

Frigg is my *fulltrúa*, my fully trusted one. There is no issue of my heart that I cannot share with her and seek her support and guidance. I connect with her as wife, mother, lady of the keep, no-nonsense organizer and planner, and as a witch and gythia. I have a permanent Frigg altar in the room I devote to the ancestors and ancestresses, and when I'm writing or when we gather for a large special occasion family meal, I always place her statue in the room. She is the heart of my heart and the heart of my home. I have aspected (a form of deity possession practiced in my Assembly of the Sacred Wheel's tradition) Frigg many times and find that her love and compassion is deep, but she will expect you to dust yourself off and get back on the proverbial horse. She is considerate and practical and her advice leans towards making a plan and finding a way. If that way is barred or peters out, find another! Frigg expects perseverance, compassion, frithfulness, courage, planning, and foresight from her followers.

Although She is far-sighted, Frigg rarely divulges the probable outcomes for choices you make or may make. Like a mother who is concerned for an adult child, and who gives advice, Frigg usually (but not always) waits until you approach her. She will often have you look more deeply into your own motivations and priorities for answers, but sheds light on the way to discernment. When I have aspected Frigg, I feel a tremendous upwelling of serenity and rootedness, but also clarity of vision, a sense of her deep wisdom, and her sharp wit and dry sense of humor. Here are some relationship questions. Feel free to take the out the word "partner" and substitute "deity":

- Do you believe there's one person you're meant to be with?
- Do you believe in wyrd/destiny?
- How do you know when you love someone?
- If you have a beloved partner, what made you fall in love with them?
- Do you feel comfortable asking your partner what made them fall in love with you? Why/Why not?
- How has your relationship changed/ grown?
- What actions do you and/or your partner need to take so that it can become stronger?
- What do you do now to nurture your relationship?
- Is love something that scares you? Why?
- Are you the bird or the hand in your relationship/s?
- Is it possible to be both the bird and the hand for each other?

Far Seeing—Wyrd Spinner—Magic Worker

Destiny is important, see, but people go wrong when they think it controls them. It's the other way around.
— Terry Pratchett, *Wyrd Sisters*

Does the walker choose the path, or the path the walker?
— Garth Nix, *Sabriel*

In *Men in Black 3*, there's a character named Griffin whose species can anticipate the infinite potential outcomes dependent on choices made in any given moment. At one point, after a satellite diverts an asteroid's path and saves earth from destruction, he sighs with relief and remarks, "That was a close one." As a great seeress, I think Frigg has felt that relief, or its opposite, countless times! As a goddess with foreknowledge, Frigg can also foresee the outcomes of our actions (perhaps in more than one dimension) and although she will support and give advice, she will not come right out and tell you the consequences of your choice. She wants us to consider our words, actions, and their consequences for ourselves. What we learn from Frigg's workings in the lore is that Frigg is very aware of the lives of the humans to whom she is connected—she will act to help us, but our deeds are our own and how we choose to shape our *ørlög*—the cards we are dealt—is largely up to us. Although she can interact with us in the moment, like all of the beings we call god/desses, she exists outside of a particular place and time and thus can see the correlation between that which is, that which is becoming, and that which will be depending upon the choices we make.

Frigg is a powerful magic worker. A truly magical act (as opposed to the illusion of a magician) occurs when someone uses their knowledge of seen and unseen forces to manifest their will in a particular working. Learning to manifest and send, say, healing energy through *galdr* or a ritual, takes training of the mind and much study, but if you seek healing (for example), or have consented to have this done, you can always call upon Frigg and her handmaiden Eir (the goddess of healing) to manifest that healing for you. With her twelve attendant goddesses, one could even say that she is high priestess of a coven, a theory I happen to like as I'm a witch as well as a gythia. Both Freyja and *Völuspá*'s seeress acknowledge Frigg's wisdom and sight, and though she does not speak of what she sees, she will act (as in the case of Baldr, the Langobards, or Agnar) to attain the outcome she desires. She scrys the worlds from Hlidskjálf, fares forth in her her falcon cloak to work her will, transforms her appearance, works closely with the Norns and will lend her influence through diety possession, overshadowing, and trancework. She and her designated handmaids, especially Eir, Hlin, and Syn, ward and protect women in childbirth, as Oddrun called upon Frigg to help Borgny through childbirth in the *Poetic Edda*'s *Oddrun's Lament*. Her role as a goddess of childbirth also connects her to the Norns. Her runes are both Berkano (**ᛒ**), the sheltering birch, and Perthro (**ᛈ**), the womb, the lot box, and the Well of Wyrd.

As I have discussed, it seems that Frigg may have a blind spot when it comes to the actions of the Jotnar (and specifically Loki), but maybe it is that she perceives many possible outcomes which are dependent on the actions of others in a particular moment. Maybe she has no choice, once that moment has passed and choices have been made, to attempt to turn the wyrd that those actions dictate (as she does in the case of Baldr). Odin consults the völva regarding Ragnarök, and the völva says that she sees farther than Frigg, or why would Odin have bothered to consult her when Frigg shares his bed? I believe that while Frigg's foresight is great, there are aspects that she cannot divine and cannot change, despite her best efforts. Her wisdom and foresight make her unwilling to divulge information because, ultimately, we must choose, and her interference through a direct revelation of our wyrd might make matters worse as easily as it might make matters better.

Sometimes words and deeds have more impact than we can imagine. Sometimes words and deeds change lives. Therefore, Frigg's guidance is often related to looking at oneself, knowing oneself, asking questions, and determining results for yourself. It makes good sense that She would be reticent to speak of what She sees, for words and advice have great importance. The words we speak, the orlog we lay down, are woven into the web of wyrd, usually in small but significant ways—but sometimes in ways that impact many lives and even the lives of future generations. If this is true for a mortal, how much greater the impact when a Great One like Frigg speaks her truth, gives advice, and spins threads that impact the web of wyrd?

Like Frigg, we may need to take time to pull back and see the forest instead of just the trees. You can always turn to Frigg for clarification, consult the runes, and write a pro/con list. In my experience, Frigg poses questions like the following to help you make a choice.

- How does this decision affect my life and reflect my values?
- What's motivating me to make this decision?
- What's my ideal outcome?
- What are some potential outcomes and how will I feel about them in the future?
- Will my future self be happy about this decision? Why?
- How will this decision affect other people and parts of my life?
- What would happen if I did nothing (also a choice!)?

Frigg and the Spinning of Wyrd

In *Roles of the Northern Goddess*, H. E. Davidson states that Frigg, as a weaver, spinner and the patroness of weavers and spinners, is associated with destiny (Davidson 2005, p. 121). Her connection to the three bright stars of Orion's Belt, the *Friggerock* or Frigg's Distaff, also connects Frigg to the fiber arts. One way to imagine Frigg's magical spinning is to think of the wool that has been spun into fibers as that which is (the manifested past), the wool that is running through Her fingers as that which is becoming (the constantly changing moment of present), and the unspun, carded wool as that which will be (the future). In folklore, think of Sleeping Beauty, where the good fairies and the bad fairy (like the family disir or norns) either curse or bless, and bend wyrd for the newborn princess. The spinning wheel is symbolic of wyrd, and acts like the sleep-thorn Odin used upon Brynhild in the *Völsunga saga*—another tale connected to magic, curses, and the force of wyrd (and dragons!).

In the lore, spinning is a magical act and the spindle is an instrument of magic. *Laxdaela Saga*'s Gudrún Ósvífursdóttir spins with a literal vengeance after she incites her husband, Bolli, to kill her ex-lover, Kjartan. As a goddess with foreknowledge who is connected to childbirth and naming, as is the case when she tricks Odin into renaming the Winniles the Langobards [Long Beards], Frigg is associated with naming rites and in laying down our ørlög—the parameters of our lives laid down at our birth. In this regard and in her work with wyrd, Frigg's power is connected to that of the Nornir. I cannot delve into an extended discussion of wyrd and ørlög here, but I highly recommend Patricia Lafayllve's excellent book *A Practical Heathen's Guide to Asatru* and chapter eight in particular.

- Think about how the foundations of your life were set by the time, place, and family who raised you.
- How have the choices that were made for you, and later, the choices that you have made affected your life—your wyrd?
- What does the saying, "We are our deeds," mean to you?
- How could you bend wyrd?
- Wyrd is a web—how do your choices and words affect those closest to you?

Wyrd Working

I am spinning my wyrd right now, this moment,
I am choosing my path forward, right now, this moment,
Each choice guides my direction.
I spin my thread in the great web spanning outward from
My family, my community, my country, this world.
My orlog is woven into the tapestry of this time and place.
May my choices be virtuous
May my thread be true!
          —Maire Durkan

Steadfast Spinner,
Wyrd Weaver,
Help me to look at my life's warp and weft with an artist's eyes!
Beautiful strands
Crafted and tinted by good deeds and loving words
Snarled strands
Their colors muddied by poor decisions and regret—
Both are woven into the tapestry of my life.
Help me to learn from my mistakes and to appreciate that
my thread and pattern
is part the great Web of Wyrd.
When I scry, consult the runes, use seidh, or turn to magic
may I prepare well
and make honorable choices that nourish my soul.
Although you do not speak my fate,
help me to know myself and be wise and courageous!
Where there the is a task, may I perform it well.
Where there is an opportunity, may I make the best choices.
Where there is a journey, may I complete it
and be wiser and stronger for the experience.
May I think well before taking an oath,
and may I fulfill it with honor.
Where there are puzzles,
may I have the wit and patience to solve them
May I choose a goal wisely
and may I have the courage, wit, and perseverance to achieve it
When I galdr, read runes, or journey,
When I allow You to use me as a vessel to work your will,
May my sight be true,
And may my words and deeds
Be welcome additions to the web of Wyrd.
      —Maire Durkan

Key Keeper

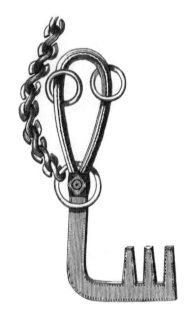

Years ago, our son Eamon made a beautiful wooden key rack where all of the keys in our house are supposed to live when not in use. It's never good when keys, especially car keys, don't return to their designated home. For most of us, the most important physical keys in our lives are probably our car keys and our house keys. In fact, when I'm out and about, I sometimes hang my car keys on a lanyard around my neck. That's about as close as I get to a Viking housewife's belt with keys attached!

Today, many of our mundane keys come in the form of passwords or finger IDs that we use to unlock accounts, documents, and websites and woe betide you if you forget or don't update your passwords! But there are also keys that unlock our heart's secrets and treasures and the doors that lead to the realms of the god/desses and the holy beings, including the landwights and our ancestors, that exist on Midgard and among the Nine Worlds. These are doors that we must unlock with knowledge and caution because they lead to realms where we will be challenged, undergo ordeals, and encounter all manner of beings, as we journey through seidh or trancework. As a gythia and witch, I have spent over a decade training, journeying, and leading people on vision quests and guided meditations as well as opening doors to the spirit realm through invocation and galdr. We must be very vigilant keepers of these keys because it's a terrible thing to be hacked, electronically or energetically. If some wight hacks our information on any plane of existence, our very identity is at stake. In her own hall, Syn guards the door, but it is Frigg who holds the keys and presides over Fensalir and Odin's halls, and indeed over the whole of Asgard. We can always call upon Frigg to help to recognize and attain the keys we need to open the doors to realms of the spirit and to call upon Syn to guard our boundaries as we fare forth and return. We can call upon Frigg to help us stay organized and be responsible and mindful keepers of the many keys in our lives.

In Medieval times, the lady of the house held the keys to the household and to all the valuables stored within—a position of great trust and responsibility. The key keeper could open and lock all doors, share precious items like spices and jewelry, welcome guests, and preside over feasts. In Viking times (CE 800-1066) keys have been found in women's graves and many scholars speculate that they were a symbol of a woman's power and status in the home and in society. The role of a woman and the symbolism of keys is even accounted in the *Poetic Edda*, in the *Lay of Thyrm (Þrymskviða)*. When Thor disguises himself as Freya and goes to wed Thrym so that he will return Mjolnir, Heimdall remarks, "Let a housewife's door keys dangle about him." It really doesn't matter whether you "run" a household, rent an apartment, or share a space with others. We are all keepers of keys—whether to websites, cars, doors, or the keys to the spirit realms. We can call upon Frigg and her handmaiden Fulla to help us to be responsible keepers of the things that we value.

- What keys are vital in your life?
- Why are they so important?
- What do you treasure? Why?
- How does their importance reflect upon your life?

Hail Lady of the Keep!
Bearer of the keys to all Asgard's treasures,
help me to be a responsible key keeper.
May I be organized and vigilant.
May I think well before I open what is locked
and may what I retrieve be well used.
May what I lock away be well guarded,
but let me not be as Fafnir
greedily hoarding what I hold dear!

Sometimes I have shared the key
To my heart—
May I share it only with those who
love truly.
May the secrets I hold
be held with right good will
and unlocked and shared only with great forethought.
And may I be a weaver of frith
in my home and in my communities.
         —Maire Durkan

Frith Weaver

Starlings on their own seem ordinary—even pesky—but in a group, a kindred of thousands called a murmuration, they become something powerful and dazzling as they cascade downwards, surge upwards, compress and distend in coordinated patterns above our heads. In this sense, a murmuration is symbolic of frith. Within a group, whether family, hearth, kindred, coven, or other, frith's energy is dynamic and interactive, with pushes, pulls, currents, ups, and downs. Frithful relationships provide needed information, support and protection when troubles arise (in whatever form they appear for you). In an atmosphere of frith, people can work through disagreements, protect each other against whatever danger threatens and work, play, and worship together with good will. Like a murmuration, frith is a relationship formed from mutual trust and respect and honorable words and deeds.

Most of us have some knowledge or experience of dysfunctional relationships and group collapse. Folk who work to build and maintain frithful relationships in their daily lives and in their communities, are much more likely to enjoy healthy, functional communities. As the greatest of frith weavers, Frigg supports and lends Her energies to building and maintaining inclusive, productive, well organized Heathen communities. She will help us to make our innangardhs, our in-yards, of blood and spirit functional. It is also Her goal to build frithful connections with other faith communities as well as with individuals who follow a solitary Northern

Tradition path. The word and the concept of frith may still be unfamiliar to you, but like the term innangarth (and frithgarth or frithstead) it is central to Heathen practice and especially to a relationship with Frigg for the very roots of Her name and frith are intertwined.

Pri, the Proto-Indo-European root of Frigg's name, can be translated as "to love" or "beloved." *Priyas*, frith's Proto-Indo-European root, can be translated as "one's own" and is also related to the words "friend" and "free" (Gundarsson, 2007, ch. 7, p. 499). Although Modern English has no single equivalent, a state of frith certainly entails harmony, peace, and concord. Frith requires the reciprocity of trust—the runic energy of Gebo (X)—a gift for a gift. To be trusted and supported, you must be trust-worthy and supportive. It's fine to have and express opposing viewpoints even when these may lead to constructive heated arguments, because a frithful relationship involves mutual respect. In the Lore, folk engage in three kinds of frithful relationships: kin frith which was frith between kin groups created through blood as well as marriage, adoption, and fostering (very common in Icelandic society of the Saga age); oath frith which created solidarity between a godhi/chieftain/ and later a king/queen between his and sometimes her (see Unn/Aud The Deep Minded) followers; and frith between a person and their gods, goddesses, and holy beings such as landwights, ancestors, Alfar (who might be ancestors or Alfs) , and the Disir.

The great warrior-poet, Egil Skallagrimson, expresses kin-frith in his poem mourning the death by drowning of his son Bodvar:

> My stock stands on the brink,
> pounded as plane-trees on the forest's rim,
> no man is glad who carries the bones
> of his dead kinsman. . .
> Harsh was the rift the wave hewed
> in the wall of my father's kin;
> I know it stands unfilled and open,
> My son's breach that the sea wrought.
> (Smiley, 2005, p. 153)

In her article, "On the Meaning of Frith," Winifred Hodge points out the difference between contemporary kin-frith and that of the frithweaver brides of the heroic era of the *Poetic Edda* and the saga eras: "They regarded the courageous act of marrying into an enemy clan as frithweaving, and so would we; but they also saw vengeance against those who broke through the boundaries of frith—outsiders who damaged their kindred in some way—as being properly supportive of frith, which we would not regard today as 'peaceful' behavior." As I discuss in my article, "The Role of Örlög, Sköp and Urðr in the Vengeance of Guðrún Gjúkadóttir," Gudrun's marriages are secondary to her obligation to uphold her frith ties to her kin (Durkan 2018). Gudrun enjoys frith, well-being and harmony, gives birth to the twins Sigmund and Svanhild, and seems to be a contented wife and mother. This period of frith ends when Sigurðr is killed by Gudrun's brothers. The frith ties of blood kin came even before her beloved husband Sigurd,z and she cannot avenge him when her brothers murder him, a situation that is unimaginable in our modern culture.

Another kind of frithful relationship is formed between chieftain and followers. In the *Havámál* (145) Odin states that a gift always looks for a gift. This sentiment is evident in in the form of sworn oaths, and the gift of gold arm rings and other gifts which sealed the bond between lord and follower. In a world where survival was far from a certainty, this mutual support (especially if augmented by a bond of kinship) was essential. This aspect of frith is expressed in *Beowulf* when Hrothgar keeps his vows and grants arm rings and riches to the men sworn to him as the feasted in his mead hall.

Another example of frith from Beowulf is Wealhtheow's role as a lady of the mead hall and keep who acts as both diplomat and peace-weaver when she gives Beowulf gifts and asks him to become her sons' counselor. Perhaps the most significant frith relationship is that which exists between you and the god/desses and holy beings you honor and/or worship. I find even a few moments of meditation each morning with Frigg and / or of her handmaidens allows me to start my day with the goal of frith in mind. We can dedicate a portion of land, of a property, and certainly of our hearts as a frithgarth/frithstead. Traditionally, a frithgarth or frithstead was an area dedicated to the god/desses and holy wights both seen and unseen. Within this space, weapons, fighting and bloodshed were forbidden. The Icelandic mountain Helgafell, translated "Helga" or holy and "fell" mountain, is an example of Viking Age Icelanders setting aside a sacred place (for Thor in this case) as a frithstead. *Eyrbyggja saga* states that Thórolfur Mostrarskegg, the region's first settler, gave the mountain its name and forbade anyone to even look at it unwashed. The significance of a frithgarth for Heathens is evidenced by an English law opposed to Heathenism which spoke against the construction of a "*fridh-geard* [fence of frith] on any man's land about a stone or tree or a spring or suchlike ungodly foolishness" (Gundarsson 2019, p. 344). Today you can hallow a piece of land as a frithstead either temporarily or permanently.

We live in a me-centered society where the individual often comes before the group, even the kin group. Still, it is a rare individual who can get very far without the support that frithful relationships provide. Heathens frequently say, "We are our deeds." Frigg teaches us that frith require mindful choices and mindful actions if we are to maintain functioning healthy relationships with kith and kin. Frith is part of ensuring the welfare of the real-world associations that we have consciously constructed. Frith's energy is the active energy of the rune Gebo (ᚷ) which represents an equal exchange given with good will. Whether it's a place to stay, a meal provided, ears to listen, arms to hug, responsibilities honored, or a group of like-minded folk with whom you can worship, frithful acts, build frithful relationships and communities. Almost no one exists in complete isolation from others and, if you are Heathen, your community and the bond of frith woven between its members is of the greatest consequence.

Before beginning the devotions, take some time to define what frith means to you and how you act frithfully within your communities. To return to the metaphor of the starlings, as we support and adjust to each other within the bond of frith, we can achieve more than we could possibly achieve alone. If you'd like to explore this topic further, I've included meditations on frith in the Rituals and Meditations chapter of this devotional.

Hail to you Frigg!
Key Keeper, Frith weaver,
May I greet this day with gratitude.
May I be a frith worker and weaver.

May I be compassionate to those who cross my path
and find a kind, work, act, or gesture
to offer them.
May I know joy and find joy
May the energies of Wunjo and Mannaz
Flow through me.
             —Maire Durkan

Rune Warden—Secret Keeper

> The runes you must find and the meaningful letter,
> a very great letter,
> a very powerful letter,
> which the mighty sage stained
> and the powerful gods made
> and the runemaster of the gods carved out. . .

> Do you know how to carve, do you know how to interpret,
> do you know how to stain, do you know how to test out,
> do you know how to ask, do you know how to sacrifice,
> do you know how to dispatch, do you know how to slaughter?
> — *Rúnatal*, from *Hávamál* (transl. Larrrington)

My first encounters with runes occurred around the age of twelve, courtesy of J.R.R. Tolkien. As a huge fangirl, I wanted to learn more and, although I didn't realize it at the time, those were my first steps on the rune road. Over thirty years later, when I began my journey into Heathenism, I studied the runes in earnest. One word really did begin to lead to another; I took workshops, read many books including Diana Paxson's *Taking Up the Runes* and Kveldulf Gundarsson's *Teutonic Magic,* both of which I highly recommend. Many years into this journey, after I realized that I was a Friggswoman and dedicated myself to Her, she prompted me to go further and actually lead a study group using Diana Paxson's *Taking Up the Runes,* Kveldúlfr Gundarsson's *Teutonic Magic,* and Edred Thorsson's *Futhark: A Handbook of Rune Magic.* [NB: Although Thorsson is controversial and I don't agree with his views, this is, IMHO, a good book.]

Frigg's prompts to undertake this work were gentle but firm. As I was still in the midst of raising our very large family, homeschooling, and immersed in my mundane and spiritual commitments, I didn't feel confident that this was something that I could do. During a trance journey I took to Fensalir, as I carded wool while Frigg spun, she told me to carry on with this work and the folk who were called to this journey would come. So, I had my own Field of Dreams to manifest. More to support me (or so they thought!) than out of a huge desire to study runes, five

Frigg and her maidens, envisioned by Carl Doepler (1874).

of my friends—all witches—embarked on this two-year journey with me. It transformed us all and I speak for all of us when I say that together we took up the runes more deeply that we could have ever imagined possible. Two became very skilled with the runes as a tool of divination (only one aspect of how they can be used) and very connected to Odin, one to Tyr, and all have relationships with Frigg. Some have additional relationships with her handmaidens and all have become frithweavers who use the runes and runic energy in their magickal and healing work. They all walk the rune road, continue to study and be proactive, and develop unique relationships with the Æsir, Ásynjur, and holy wights.

The word *rune* can be translated as secret or mystery. Just as Her handmaiden, Fulla, keeps Frigg's secrets, Frigg keeps Odin's. She also keeps hidden the mysteries of that which should be (i.e. the future) and is both a guardian and guide to the energies and mysteries of the multiverse as expressed through the runes. The runic energies run throughout the multiverse. Each being contains currents that connect to these forces. We can call upon Frigg to support us as we learn how to connect to and express these forces.

The rune road is not an easy path. Odin hung for nine nights, pierced himself, and was reborn in order to gain this wisdom. In terms of suffering in order to gain wisdom, Odin expects no less of His followers. However, if we invite Frigg into our lives, she will guide us and tempers this journey with her energies and the support of her handmaidens.

Homemaker—Joy of Kindred

> *The ornament of a house is the friends who frequent it.*
> — *Ralph Waldo Emerson*

There was a time, not too long ago, when many folk were pretty dismissive of homemakers. In the binary era a homemaker might be put down as a "house mouse," taken for granted as a "housewife," or disparaged as a "house husband." Some of that prejudice still exists. Please know that being a homemaker is honorable, sacred, hard work that honors Frigg, the ancestors, and the landwights and housewights, and blesses you, your family and your guests. If you approach your tasks mindfully, the duties of a homemaker are a beautiful way to honor Frigg.

A homemaker is a multitasker who must know how to budget, plan and prepare meals, do and delegate chores, be security guard, counselor, and a host of other personalized roles. Many of us work outside of the home and have to juggle that part of our lives as well. If you have kids or fur babies, add outings, doctor's visits, being supportive in hundreds of little and big ways and doing whatever is needed to keep the home from imploding—or exploding. One of the most fulfilling ways that we can be a joy to our kith and kin is to provide a warm and welcoming environment where folk can come together, relax and enjoy each other's company.

As the patroness of homemakers, Frigg appreciates a tidy home and most definitely a tidy altar (that includes dusting her statue). As a goddess of frith she also expects us to honor our housewights and landwights appropriately and keep their offerings fresh. Despite our best efforts, life sometimes gets in the way of mopping, vacuuming, and dish washing, but we can still be organized and make an effort to manifest a clean, safe, welcoming home where folk feel loved, accepted, and cared for. I take pride in homemaking because every meal cooked, towel folded, counter wiped, and ward reinforced is an act of love that supports my family and honors Frigg. Frigg places great values in the little acts that add up and make a home a place of frith. My children and my husband also contribute to the mundane tasks that make the home welcoming and to the extent that they fulfill that role, they too are homemakers.

When someone is hurting, the home should be a place of solace and refuge—not a place to be avoided at all costs. Therefore, part of a home-maker's job is to know how to ward their home both in a physical sense (clean surfaces against the microscopic icks, and motion detectors, security systems, and good locks against the bigger ones) and on a spiritual level (against baneful wights) with wards and purification. A ward is a protective spell/rune/ symbol that repels baneful wights. Some examples are purification through galdring, smudging (I use white sage), a singing bowl or bells, or sweeping with a broom, inscribing the Elhaz rune or a bind rune on entryways, or placing a Pennsylvania Deitsch "hex" sign on your house. I mark my doors with a charged Elhaz (ᛉ) which I periodically recharge, and routinely smudge, galdr, and energetically sweep my home (best performed with windows open). Like routine house cleaning, routine warding is a vital aspect of homemaking to keep baneful beasties from your home. You can also call upon Syn to guard your property's boundaries and your house and land wights to aid in home warding and patrolling the grounds.

The Homemaker and Land and House Wights

As Heathens and folk on a Northern Tradition path, we recognize sentient beings—*landvættir* or landwights and *húsvættir* or housewights who share our homes with us. They too must be cherished and cared for. I have designated a stone near my upstairs and downstairs stoves and invited our housewight to live there. In the back of our garden, I have a shrine to Nerthus and the landwights. In both cases, I regularly leave gifts such as beer, mead, etc. or honey and milk, flowers, a pretty stone or jewelry. When I hold rites and blóts on my property I always ask leave of the wights, invite their protection, and include them in libations from the blót bowl. You can avoid a great deal of harm if you are on good terms with your housewights and landwights. I was once warned of an electrical fire that I would never have suspected had I not been "prodded" to go into our basement and take a look at our circuit box! In a world where climate change is a reality, we can honor our local wights and the great ones even more by practicing a greener and more sustainable homemaking. We can all buy more products from local growers, recycle, be aware of energy usage, pick products with less plastic, and cook more plant-based meals which are less taxing on the environment.

In the 21st century, the word homemaker is inclusive. Whether you are a stay-at-home parent doing the vital work of raising children or someone who takes pride in the time and effort needed to maintain a welcoming home, we can all find worth in our contributions to our households and to the environment.

Questions:

- Do you consider yourself a 'homemaker? Why or why not?
- What does the term homemaker mean to you?
- Frigg is a goddess of the hearth and home. How can you honor her in your daily tasks on the home front?
- Do you honor your house wight/s and land wights? How might you deepen those relationships?
- What makes a home a special place for you?
- What things can you do to make your home that special place?

Care Taker—Wise Protectress

In the mythology and in our lives, Frigg has always been a protectress. One of Frigg's few praise names in the lore is Hlín—which is often translated as protection. Not only is she called Hlín, Frigg has a handmaiden named Hlín who is charged with protecting those under her care. Frigg takes good care of those under her mantle. As the prescient CEO of Asgard, Frigg uses resources at her disposal, including her handmaidens to manifest her goals. Her handmaidens Hlín, whose name means "protection," and Syn, whose name means "denial," extend and manifest Frigg's protective nature. As followers of Frigg, we can always call upon her protective energies, but she also expects us to stand up for ourselves and

44

learn from our mistakes and past experiences, so that we become mindful protectors of our homes, families, kindreds, caretakers of the environment.

Warding

Whether in the home, car, office, or other personal space, we can call upon Frigg and her handmaidens Syn and Hlín in the warding and protection of our boundaries and places of refuges. One way to protect is to walk the bounds of your property and call upon their protection. I trace Elhaz or a bindrune in red energy upon my office, car, and household doors and/or windows and ask Frigg, Hlín, and Syn and to guard my boundaries in conjunction with the landwights and housewights of that spot. It's always advisable to offer gifts of food, drink, or even energy to the wights, but in return for Frigg's protection, I offer her the careful maintenance of my home, yard, or personal space and promise to be a good caretaker of the beings seen and unseen under my care (that includes chickens, cats, and plants).

If you call upon Frigg and her handmaidens for support, you had best have the space clean and organized. As above, so below and as within, so without; dirt and disorganization attract unwelcome visitors both seen (mice, bugs, germs) and unseen (the unwanted bale-working wights attracted to chaos and upset). We want to start our warding on the right foot and make the space as unattractive as possible to unwelcome guests!

Always keep Frigg's altar tidy, make sure any offerings are fresh, and give her the gifts of devotion and industriousness. For my garden, I've created a bindrune combining Elhaz (ᛉ, the spikey snowflake of protection), Fehu (ᚠ, fertility and abundance), and Berkano (ᛒ, which is a great goddess rune of protection, strength, and flexibility). It doesn't hurt to use smoke or incense to purify a space (if possible, open windows) and using a broom (any will do, but birch is the best) to sweep the negative energy out of a space chanting something like:

> *Gracious Ladies, bless this garth*
> *With strong defenses and frith-filled hearth!*
> *Frigg, Hlín, Syn*
> *Protect these bounds—*

North, East, South, West, within, without!
Bless all that enter—kin, guests, and friends
May our good fortune never end!
I welcome wights of weal to stay
and banish baneful wights away!
    —Maire Durkan

Lady of the Disir

Matronae from a Romano-Germanic altar, Nettersheim, Germany. Image by Kleon3. CC BY-SA 4.0.

In the early dark of a cold Solstice eve, a hearth fire glows brightly casting warmth and light upon the folk gathered together on Mother's Night. We gather to honor our mothers still with us and our Disir mortal and immortal—the women of our ancestral lines who have elected to watch over us. Photographs, favorite foods, and items that were made by or belonged to beloved women, surround a statue of Frigg and another of the Matronae—three seated women/ goddesses wearing headdresses who were venerated at least since the 1st century AD in Germanic cultures, connected to protection of the family, fertility, and childbirth (Simek 2007, p. 204). Each of us holds a candle. The gythia lights her candle and begins to relate her family line and thanks these women for their sacrifices and their lives. She says, "We are all sparks of your flames." As the light is passed as the spark of life was passed generation to generation, each person speaks of their lineage and connections and the once darkened room become bright with the light of many candle flames.

Whether still living or passed on, a Dis (or the Anglo-Saxson *ides/ idis*) is a kinswoman. As is pointed out in *Our Troth*, although disir/idis-es may refer to clan mothers who have passed and who "still guard their descendants and help them in various ways," the term can refer to living women, and "the two have basically the same might, though the dead ones, dwelling wholly in the hidden realms, are thought to be stronger in matters of magic" (Vol. 1, p. 439). Mother's Night is one of my favorite holy tides because it connects us to the women of our ancestral line and to ancestresses of spirit as well as of DNA. Frigg is Dis of the Æsir as Freyja is Dis of the Vanir, and we can call upon Her as All-Mother to watch over and protect us. Egill Skalla-Grimsson's "Sonatorrek" names the Æsir "Frigg's descendants," but we too are her descendants. In sagas such as Snorri's *Ynglinga saga* and the *Saga of Hervor and King Heidrek* and *Viga-Glúms saga,* as well as in *Grímnismál,* the Disir are honored at Disablót/Disting which can be at the beginning of February, while Mother's Night (OE *Modraniht*) was held in December by the Anglo-Saxons. Rudolf Simek states that, as a Germanic sacrificial festival, Mother's Night should be associated with the Matron cult of the West Germanic peoples on the one hand, and to the *dísablót* and the Disting already known from medieval Scandinavia on the other hand, and "is chronologically to be seen as a connecting link between these Germanic forms of cult" (Simek 2007, p. 220).

> *Asadís,*
> *Fully Trusted One,*
> *Wyrd weaver,*
> *Cast your mantle of protection over me*
> *Guide and guard me*
> *As I journey through this life*
> *And may the mothers of my blood and spirit*
> *Ward my way.*
> *Hail Frigg!*
> —Maire Durkan

Caregiver

I wipe the last of the shaving cream from my father's face and hand him a warm, moist washcloth (he still wanted to do as much as he could and I wanted to give him that dignity).

"All finished! What would you like to do now?"

My father grins. "My talking books!"

In his mid-80s my father went completely blind, suffered from severe arthritis, heart disease, and finally cancer. As a decorated Pearl Harbor survivor who suffered from PSTD, he had much to cope with—his writing and poetry, and his many years giving back as a high school teacher and union leader, were all outlets that helped him process and slowly heal. He was a fabulous dad and caregiver who always made sure that my sister, brother and I were well provided for on a teacher's salary. My dad was always a caregiver to me, and even more so when my mother—his beloved wife—died from cancer when I was fourteen.

In a time when single parenting by a man wasn't a "thing," he did a great job of raising me solo. Although he wasn't Heathen, my father was the one who introduced me to the god/desses of Norse mythology. No one could have coped with the difficulties of old age and met his death with more courage and dignity, and it was my very great honor to be his caregiver. Being a caregiver is an honor, but when you have many other obligations beyond your role as caregiver, you feel squeezed and stressed. Frigg will support all caregivers and watch over you as you go about your tasks. We can also call upon Eir and Hlín for personal healing, strength, and comfort.

Frigg has experienced the highs and lows of caring for others. She will fight to the finish, but knows there is also a time to delegate and finally to let go. When wyrd can't be turned—call upon her and her handmaidens for comfort and discernment of a way forward. She is a compassionate goddess and a caregiver not just to women and women in childbirth, but to all who genuinely need her comfort and sincerely call upon her for aid and solace. I have found her support to be steady and true, not dramatic (even when my personal life is fraught with drama). She will help you to hold the fort, to stay focused and organized when that is necessary, and to be a compassionate caregiver. She makes it quite clear that we are not to be martyrs or doormats—we must care for ourselves as well, and must seek help for ourselves before we find that we don't have the resources to cope and are on the verge of emotional and physical collapse. Frigga delegates responsibility to goddesses who are competent in various fields and not only should we call upon Hlín, Eir, our ancestors, or other spiritual sources of aid, we should seek the manifest help we need on Midgard to be good caregivers for ourselves and for others. As Frigg has a team, you should seek out people who can relieve so that you can care for yourself.

- Do you think you're being selfish when you put your needs first? Why or why not?
- Do you have trouble asking for what you need? Why or why not?
- As a caregiver to folk of any age, do you feel that you must prove that you are worthy? Do you do too much as a result?
- How do your oaths affect your role as a caregiver? For example, if you promised that you would always care for your mother, brother, etc., does your oath make you solely responsible for that person or are there others who can step in?
- Do you believe that if you don't do the task, no one will?
- Which of Frigg's handmaidens could you call upon for aid? What would you ask of them?

Wise Protectress
Help me to trust your good counsel
Help me to do what is necessary
For myself and for my loved ones
Help me to stand by my oaths
And take joy in my tasks
Let me have perseverance,
But let me also care for myself
Let me identify problems,
Seek solutions,
Ask for help and accept
The right help.
Lady of frith and community
Help me to use the resources in my community
To care for myself and others.
　　　　—Maire Durkan

Chapter 4: Songs, Poems, and Prayers

Formal or informal, sung, spoken, whispered, or offered in the heart's silence, prayer is an active heartfelt desire to reach out to the Great Ones—to speak our heart's truth and to listen. The ways we choose to make that connection are quite personal and all of the offerings in this section are prayers in various forms. There are as many ways to pray as there are individuals. Laughter with friends and joy in a beautiful aspect of nature can also be forms of prayer. No matter its emotion or intent, when we lift our hearts and thoughts up to the god/desses and weal-working wights, our words and thoughts connect to the sacred.

Fricka and Freia as envisioned by Carl Doepler,
in his costume designs for *Der Ring des Nibelungen* (1876)

Invocation to Frigg

By Maire Durkan

Frigga, Frigga
All Mother—Queen Beloved
Folk: We call to you

Frigga, Frigga
Key Keeper, Peace-weaver
Folk: We call to you

From the Marsh Hall
Folk: Come to us
From the High Seat
Folk: Come to us
From the hearth's warmth
Folk: Come to us
From the heart's core
Folk: Come to us.

Frigga Frigga
Far seeing—Wyrd Spinner
Folk: We call to you
Frigga, Frigga
Rune Warden, Secret Keeper
Folk: We call to you

From the Marsh Hall
Folk: Come to us
From the High Seat
Folk: Come to us
From the hearth's warmth
Folk: Come to us
From the heart's core

Frigga, Frigga
Homemaker—Joy of Kindred
Folk: We call to you

Frigga, Frigga
Caretaker, Wise Protectress
Folk: We call to you

From the Marsh Hall
Folk: Come to us
From the High Seat
Folk: Come to us
From the Hearth's Warmth
Folk: Come to us
From the Heart's core
Folk: Come to us
Frigga, Frigga

"Dreams Sung True" Song #20.
https://www.youtube.com/watch?v=bugAzHndoKQ

Fensalir Song

By Diana Paxson

Between the worlds with spirit sight,
The geese are crying—
Women together wearing white
We wend from Midgard through the night
The reeds are sighing—
Landwights bless the way we go,
The geese are crying—
Disir help your children grow
for Women's wisdom we would know,
The reeds are sighing—
Long lost the path that we would find,
The geese are crying—
Through trackless marsh our way we wind
With hallowed heart and mirthful mind,
The reeds are sighing—
Among salt-meadows stands a hall,
The geese are crying—
Strength and grace in every wall
And room within to welcome all,
The reeds are sighing—
All hail the queen who rules within,
The geese are crying—
She takes the twisted fates we spin
And weaves us all into one kin,
The reeds are sighing—

Prayer to Frigg

By Diana Paxson

From the darkness of earth you arise,
Fjorgvin's first daughter,
Bending like the birch tree
at the bounds of the glacier.
You are the stillness at the heart of the world,
you are its silence.
Rams with white fleeces
roam free round your dwelling:
In your hall stands a loom;
Norns spin the thread for your weaving.
It is warped with the fates of the world,
Only you see the pattern.
You sit at the head of the hearth,
twelve maidens blaze around you,
Sparks spun from your brightness.
In their faces you are reflected;
You are all the women of all the worlds,
you are the Beloved.
Giver of Law are you,
and High Seat of Sovereignty.
Allfather counsels kings,
but it is you who choose them.
You teach magic to queens;
you give names to the nations.
Golden the god you gave birth to,
but Laufey's child betrayed him.
Your son will return
when all else you love is ended,
All this you know,
but you say nothing.

All-mother, around your altar now we are gathered,
Women together, wanting your wisdom,
Holy one hearken, hasten to help us.
These are the faces of the goddess
candles lit from her hearthfire,
water flowing from her well:
Saga. . . who knows the names of the ancestors and all the old
    tales;
Eir. . . the silent, child of Audhumla, ancient healer;
Gefion. . . who gives before we even know our need;
Fulla. . . who guards the secret of the mysteries;
Sjofn. . . the one who inclines the heart to love;
Lofn. . . giving us permission to follow our dreams;
Syn. . . our advocate, who wards the doors we need to close;
Hlin. . . the protector who shields us from harm;
Var. . . who hears all oaths by the holy hearth;
Vor. . . who knows all secrets, expanding awareness;
Snotra. . . the wise one, who always knows what to do;
Gná. . . who soars high carrying Frigg's words throughout the
    worlds.

For Frigg

By Jennifer Lawrence

They call me the Lady of the Keys;
I keep my ways,
keep myself to myself,
and all that is in my keeping
is never more secure
than when only I know why the doors are locked,
what the secrets are behind each one,
and which key opens which portal.

They call me the Weaver;
with my distaff I control the threads of warp and weft,
catching up the fabric of the future
in the tapestry I create;
you think the cloth is merely full of pretty pictures
— or not-so-pretty ones —
but in those skeins of thread and their patterns
I can see all of existence.

They call me Baldr's mother;
as if to be the creator of a child is such a small thing,
as if anyone can do it;
giving half of your essence to make a new being
is an act of magic and miracle,
and the love involved in doing so is a force of such ferocity
that, to protect him, I was willing to wring oaths
from all of reality;
the pain of my failure is a wound
that will be with me forever;
some days I walk as one already dead.

You may know my stories,
you may collect lost baby teeth, spindles, and old keys,
but some doors only I can open;
some looms will only work for me;
and some children are all the more dear
for having been loved and lost.

In my hands, I hold
the sanctity of home and hearth,
all that was and all that will be,
and the heart of every mother grieving for a fallen child.

Those who dismiss me merely as "Odin's housewife"
do so at their peril,
and I encourage those who do
to reveal their folly;
such misguided and stupid braggadocio
such dismissal of the power that I hold
— such blatant impiety —
is met with its own reward in time.

If you would, instead, honor me,
care well for the things in your keeping:
your secrets, your future, your children,
for in those things are treasure beyond gold and diamonds,
but also in those things exist
the essence and best blossoms
of all that shall ever be.

For Mothers' Night

Sung to the tune of "Silent Night"

By Maire Durkan

Peaceful night, Mothers Night
Beloved women, shining bright
Heartbeat to heartbeat, an unbroken song
Wisdom given and love passed on
Guide our way, help us grow
Guide our way, help us grow.

Wonderous night, Mothers Night
Seen and unseen, guiding lights
Mortal, immortal we honor you here
For your journeys, your laugher, your tears
Praise our blessed Disir
Praise our blessed Disir.

Silent Night Holy Night
All is calm, all is bright
Lives made beautiful through your deeds,
Hands that worked to fulfil others' needs
Mothers Dear fill this space
And bless us all with your grace.

Morning Prayer to Frigg

By Maire Durkan

Hail Frigg!
Hail to Day!
Bright song of the morning,
I begin this day with gratitude for these blessings:
    (name your blessings)
Please, give me the courage and perseverance to face any obstacles.
May I be a sower of frith
and may the work I do and the words I speak
in some small way
make my world a better place.

Evening Prayer to Frigg

By Maire Durkan

Hail Frigg!
As I enter Nótt's realm,
may my sleep bring
healing and peace.
Protect my dream journeys
and may I remember that which I am meant to recall.
Great Weaver,
weave your protection around me!
May the warp and the weft of my dreams
be wholesome and may no baneful wight enter into my dream
    garth
I thank you for your guidance and protection.

Prayer for Discernment and Self Knowledge

By Maire Durkan

Frigg bless and guide my journey of self-discovery!
Wryd Spinner,
help me hold and consider the threads of my being,
the orlog that impels me,
from its deepest roots.
Help me discern and test the fibers of my choices
And to consider and untangle their significance
before I twist then into words and deeds.
Help me to learn from my mistakes
and to accept imperfections that cannot be changed.
Wyrd Weaver,
may I journey mindfully,
may I be open
to newly revealed truths, patterns, beliefs, values
and ways of being.
When I am challenged,
before jumping to conclusions and reacting out of habit,
 may I look at both the warp and weft of a situation
to better understand its weave.
May the dark dyes of anger, anguish, hatred, and despair
be scarce
and bright, faithful threads be abundant!
I am your child—
A strand of your weaving—
May the web of my life reflect the strength and beauty of that
    connection.

Prayer to Frigg for Magical Might

By Maire Durkan

Holy Lady of Hearth Magic,
Mistress of Falcon Form,
High Soaring One,
Scryer from the High Seat,
Lift my spirit that I may soar
and travel to my desired destination!
May my mind's eye be keen and fully focused!
Keeper of the keys,
unlock my perception!
Rune Warden,
help me to discern the mysteries I seek to understand.

Parent's Prayer

By Maire Durkan

All Mother
Hearth Mother
You know the laughter, joys, and tears of parenthood,
Help me to find joy in my parenting
Help me to celebrate the small tender moments—giggles, snug-
gles, a book read together—
May I always be aware that each small act of love
leads to the milestones of first words, first steps to independence,
first friendships, and first loves.
When I feel tired, isolated, overwhelmed, irritated, and unappre-
ciated
Help me to know that raising another person
to be a strong, confident, loving adult
is the most important work that I will ever do.
Help me to lay down orlog that provides a firm foundation
from which my beloved child can fare forth into the world.
May my words and deeds
form a beautiful pattern in the web of their wyrd.

Artist's Prayer

By Maire Durkan

Cloud Spinner,
Wyrd Weaver,
Lady of Crafts,
Dis of All Artists,
May the work of my hands be sure and may it reflect my vision
Help me to learn from my mistakes.
Spark my imagination!
Let us take this journey together
Stroke by stroke
Thread by thread
Word by word
Piece by piece.
Lady of intuition and awareness,
guide my process.
May your creativity touch me
sparking my own
into a flame
leaping from my mind to my hands
from my spirit to my work.

Working Parent's Prayer to Frigg

By Maire Durkan

All Mother
Lady of Frith
Protectress and defender of children
Watch over and protect my child
As I entrust them into the care of another.
May their caregiver treat them with love, compassion, and atten-
    tiveness
Let me have no regrets
Let me be proud of the work that I do
For my work is necessary for the good of my family.
Loving Mother of All,
watch over my child
until I return.

Prayer for Fertility and a Healthy Birth

By Maire Durkan

> Lady of Berkano,
> Great goddess of fertility and protection,
> Holy One hear me!
> You know how I long for a child
> to cherish, love, and raise responsibly.
> Bless my womb
> as you blessed the womb of King Rerir's wife
> with an apple of fertility
> that I may conceive and give birth to a healthy child.
> Shelterer,
> may my womb provide perfect shelter
> and when my baby is born, may my arms,
> my deeds, and my very life provide shelter for this beloved child!
> Guide me to healthy choices
> and pour your blessings upon this conception, pregnancy, and
> birth.
> So that this beloved child inherits a strong hamingja as well as
> loving parents.

Business Blessing

By Maire Durkan

Lady of Fehu and forethought,
Focused leader and director,
Wyrd-wise Counselor,
Grant me the wisdom, discipline, honor, and perseverance
I need to make my business successful.
You who oversee the running of Asgard and the work of your
    handmaidens,
help me to discern between good and bad choices
so that my business flourishes.
May it benefit my family and my employees.
May our work fulfil our customers' needs.
Great strategist,
help me to find the best ways to reach those who will benefit from
    my products and services.
Bless my work and the work of my employees.
May it be true and sure.
May my success be gained through excellent work and honorable
    deeds.
Lady of Fehu may my business be prosperous.
Lady of Wunjo may my business bring joy.
Lady of Frith may we work together to build a supportive efficient
    work environment.

Earth Blessing

By Maire Durkan

Fjörgynn's Maid,
Earth wise Lady of the Ásynjur,
Bless this earth and all good wights that dwell here.
Bless the animals, plants, and trees,
The stones and water deep beneath my feet,
And fill this land with health and peace.
May Frith blossom here.
Heal any hurts to this space.
Protect this space.
All ill dispel
And ward it from woe-working wights!
Help me to be a good tenant and caretaker of this space.
May your might rise up out of the wilderness that was
And bless this land
With the song of your being!

Marriage / Handfasting Prayer

By Maire Durkan

Lady of Troth,
bless this couple
as they begin their journey together.
You, whose very name is Beloved,
bless them
as they step forth
determined,
united,
and linked by bonds of love.
Give them clear sight
and good fortune
Lady of Wunjo
Give them joy and passion.
May they open like blossoms!
May they blaze like fire!
For —more than blood and bone—
they are children of the Well and the Tree.
May the garth they make be blessed and bountiful
And may their hearth fire dance with frith!

Cry for Consolation After Loss

By Maire Durkan

Death's hawk-fast talons struck.
Now, the plumage of her life
is strewn on the earth.
All that shaped her
loosened, scattered, and lifted on the wind.
I touch her shirt—her book—
the silence breaks my heart.
Her laughter and music still ring in my mind.
How then can I continue
when my life is broken and scattered?
Loving Hlín,
Lady of Consolation,
Fierce Mother
who fought so hard to save your son,
Grieving Mother
who risked everything to bend Baldr's wyrd,
teach me how to bear the burden of this loss!
My soul is rent.
I do not see a way forward
and yet I must go on.
Wrap me in your mantle.
Hold me while I grieve
for you understand
that I am not yet ready to soar above it.
I am too lost.
You whisper, "Your grief is a way to heal. It is the way through."
Support me as I journey
through this dark and barren land
to a place where I may walk in joy again
recalling with love that which is
and delighting again in that which is becoming.

Prayer for Warriors

By Maire Durkan

Lady of the Disir and Norns
Guard the warriors faring forth
Guard them on all paths they tread
Above, below
East, west, south, north.
Surround them with your mantle bright
Shield them by day and guard by night
May their cause be just
And their courage strong
May their bravery be remembered long.
May they return to loved ones' arms
Strong and secure—safe and unharmed.
Please heal all wounds conflict imparts
Of mind and body,
Soul and heart,
And if in the battle they should fall,
Tenderly lift them to sacred halls.

Prayer to Frigg For Honorable and Just Leaders

By Maire Durkan

Asgard's Shining Queen,
Beloved Bridge between Asgard and Midgard.
You who sit in counsel before the Well of Wyrd,
May we choose leaders with vision and foresight.
May our leaders have the wit, will, and wisdom
To negotiate the many pitfalls and divisions of our political land-
    scape.
Astute Lady,
Far Seeing One,
Great Strategist,
You who have contended with Odin
in the field of politics and won the day,
lend Your energy to the forces of Honor and Justice!
May we the people choose leaders
who place the wellbeing of their country before their party.
May they hold their oaths as sacred
and be filled with hope, creativity, and endurance so that
the bonds they forge in our nation and among nations bring ben-
    efit and lasting peace.
Fjörgynn's Daughter,
Birch Bright All Mother,
may they honor the Earth.
May our leaders and our citizens work for ways to prevent its fur-
    ther destruction!
Lady of Frith,
may we choose those
who truly honor and respect our diversity
while recognizing our potentials as individuals
to work weal in this world.
Wyrd Spinner,
Wyrd Weaver,

through our choices—
through our deeds—
may we all work towards making our nation
a garth of liberty and justice for all.

Frigg and Freyja's daughter Gersimi, as envisioned by Lorenz Frølich (1845).
Courtesy of the National Library of Denmark.

Boast to Frigg

By Maire Durkan

I hail the Lady of Foresight
Wise Counselor
Advocate, Advisor, Arbiter!
Holy High One,
I sing your praises.
Lady of Earth,
Lady of the stars,
Lady of Liminal Places,
Wyrd Weaver,
Asa Dis,
Oaths you hear,
Orlog impart!
Constant Companion,
what would Odin be without
Your love, Your wit, Your, guidance, and Your guile?
You are solid earth to his wild wind.
Beloved Queen,
You are the hub and focal point
You are Asgard's Heart!
Lady of Frith
I praise you for your compassion, care, and considered counsel!
I praise you for opening my eyes
to the joys of hearth and home
and to the mindful management of my life.
Hail Frigg!

Chapter 5: Meditations and Rituals

There are as many ways to connect to the holy beings we honor as there are individuals, but a well-wrought ritual or meditation is a reliable way to establish relationships. Meditation is a way to listen to the God/desses and other wights (such as Alfar, Disir, and home and landwights). For some people, devotion will only be used in a ritual context, while for others rituals and meditations become a daily practice as part of solitary devotional work.

An altar to Frigg need not be elaborate, but it should be kept dusted and tidy. I bring my statue of Frigg into the midst of whatever family event is going on; if folk there aren't Heathen or Pagan, they usually don't notice the statue or think it's just a neat sculpture. She is on a side table during holidays and celebrations, and on the kitchen table when I'm writing. During blóts, when her images and statue are on an altar, the settings is much more elaborate. But generally, Frigg's altar is a half-moon table in our front room which is also dedicated to the ancestors. I like to have a fresh bouquet of flowers there and keep a small drawstring bag with any object or written intention I am placing before Her there as well. Folk who come in from outside of the tradition feel the warmth and the welcome without having to know anything specific (unless they ask) while folk in a Heathen or Pagan tradition feel Frigg's presence and may honor her. In my experience, Frigg is not a goddess who expects an opulent altar and lavish offerings. Below I've listed some of the items I use and have used on Frigg's altar. It's fine if your images and objects differ due to your scholarship, preferences, and personal experiences with Frigg.

Some of the things that I place on Frigg's altar:

- Statue or image of Frigg.
- White or blue altar cloth/s and candles.
- Blue or white fresh flowers, or a wetland arrangement with cattails.
- Images/statues of water birds such as a heron or an osprey (for me, Frigg's falcon cloak has osprey feathers).

- Garden herbs (especially herbs, like motherwort, that are connected to a feminine healing—also Frigg's connection to the fertile earth).
- Apples (as a symbol of fertility, not eternal youth—-that's Idunna's department).
- A piece of birch wood or bark (symbolic of Berkano).
- The runes Berkano (ᛒ, Frigg's rune) and Othala (ᛟ, hearth, home, ancestors), Fehu (ᚠ, good fortune), Laguz (ᛚ, water/Fensalir/birth/healing), Perthro (ᛈ, the womb, the lot box, and connections to the Norns).
- Baked goods and/or pastries (preferably home-baked—things you've made with your own hands).
- Sweet wine (like plum wine) or melomel (mead made with fruit).
- An old-fashioned key or set of keys looks best, but modern keys on a lanyard or keychain also work (Frigg as goddess of the home and keeper of the mysteries).
- Unspun wool.
- A drop spindle, with or without spun wool.
- An image of a loom or a small (very small!) replica.
- A birch broom or besom (symbolic of a tidy home).
- Crown (symbol of sovereignty).
- Image of sheep and/or rams (rams pull her chariot and She spins with wool).

Friday—Frigg's Day Rite Before Her Altar

This is a simple, straightforward rite for weekly devotions. Focus on your breath and feel yourself connected to the earth. Let go of any troubles with each breath until you are grounded and focused in this moment of devotion.

Clear the space of any unwanted noise, distractions, and ward with spirals (a symbol of Frigg's spinning in all directions and above and below) asking for Syn to guard the boundaries.

Hail Frigg! High Holy One!
Grant me the focus and stillness of the heron
That I may be with you now!
Goddess of fireside and home,
Teach me the lessons of commitment and contentment,
Service and celebration.
Warm me within and without.
I light this candle in offering to you (*light a votive candle*)
And praise you on your name day.

If there is something that you need to bring before Frigg, do so now. End with:

I ask for your guidance and support in this matter.
Thank you for your time with me. Hail Frigg!

Frigg, Goddess of Home

To bring Frigg's blessings into your home, light a candle to her each day with this invocation. Offerings of good bread, pastry, plum wine or mead are also suitable.

All Mother, bless my home I pray
Keep it safe by night and day
Send Syn to guard my boundaries well
No baneful wight within to dwell!
Bring frith and fortune to all within
And warmest welcome for friends and kin!

Land Blessing Rite

Honoring your land and house spirits is essential to the health and protection of your garth. For this, choose an appropriate spot on your property. Pour whole milk, milk with honey, or mead/beer into a small bowl. Carry outside to the chosen spot, raise it up and say:

Hail the land wights! Guardians, I give you my gratitude and all honor! Grant peace and plenty to this place! Landvaettir, with this bowl I offer to you my continuing respect, and gratitude for your presence here! May I work with you to keep this land healthy and whole."

Libate onto the earth or place the bowl on the ground as an offering and retrieve the next day.

A similar rite can be performed for your housewight/s. I placed a large stone beside two of our woodstoves where I welcomed the wights to live, and I honor them in those locations with gifts of beer, mead, and peppermints (not sure why they like them, but they do).

Frith Meditation I: Creating a Frithstead of the Heart

It may be helpful to record these meditations ahead of time, so that you can focus on the meditations. Find a quiet place where you can sit or lie in safety and undisturbed.

Close your eyes. Breath in and out. Starting with your toes, relax your body a little more with each breath, until you are at ease. With each breath, allow all troubling thoughts to depart until you are at ease. Imagine your frithstead, a strong, safe, beautiful place of peace and protection, where the Great Ones watch over you. What does your frithstead look like? Where is it located? Now picture the faces of those, seen and unseen, you would invite into this most sacred place. Picture each face, softly say their name, and call to mind the bond between you. As you hold them in your thoughts, think about how your relationship is one of frith, and why they are worthy of entering this most sacred enclosure. Who do you welcome?

Frith Meditation II: Staking Your Claim

Close your eyes. Breathe in and out, in and out. With each exhalation, release your cares and worries, and just be in this time and place. Breath in, and with the next exhalation, imagine a root of your energy extending into the earth, past soil and stones, through water and more stone, until you sense the molten heat of Earth's core. Feel it pulse with your pulse. Now, pull some of that red Earth energy up through your feet. Draw it up into your legs, torso, down your arms and up through the crown of your head. Let it fountain out and back into the earth. You are now anchored to this time and place. Safely you will journey and safely you will return.

Imagine a path in a deep wood of ancient trees that tower above your head. It is dark beneath the leaves and night is coming on. The wind sings through the branches. Boughs toss. A storm is coming and you know that you must find shelter. Beneath your feet, you can just discern a well-trodden path. Follow it as lightning flashes, thunder rumbles, wind picks up, until the whisper of the leaves becomes the roar of the sea. You hurry along the path as best you can, wishing that you weren't alone in the depth of this great forest. Then rain hammers down until you are drenched. In your fear and loneliness, you long for others and you call out, "Please! I need help!"

As the thunder rumbles and the rain continues to lash down, you have the thought: "Don't give up. Carry on along the path."

You follow the path as it winds through the trees, and just ahead you see a hooded figure cloaked in snowy white cloak bordered in light blue. Relieved, you hurry forward. She holds out her hand. You hurry to her side and take her hand. A sudden warmth and energy surges into your palm, up your arm and throughout your body. You are warm, invigorated and safe. You know that this woman is someone, in fact Someone, that you trust completely.

"Follow me," she says, "and I'll take you to your heart's home."

As you walk along the wet path, the rain doesn't touch you or the woman. Soon the storm becomes a patter of raindrops, then the rain stops, the trees thin, and you come to a beautiful meadow. A gentle breeze brings the sweet scents of flowers and meadow grasses.

The woman reaches into a pocket in her cloak and takes out freshy cut hazel stakes, and then pushes back her hood. Her clear eyes reflect the colors of the sky and her face holds an ageless beauty. Looking into Her eyes, you know that you are in the presence of Frigg, the Lady of Frith.

She hands you the hazel stakes tied with a rough hempen cord and places her hands over yours.

"We are our deeds. Will you go forward and build your frithstead, or return through the wood to the place from whence you came—to return—perhaps—another time."

You answer and make your choice.

(If you choose to return, thank Frigg for her guidance and return through the woods to the path's beginning, and begin to ground yourself and wake to the mundane world.)

You accept the hazel stakes and a wooden mallet.

"Bless these hands that do the work of frithweaving. Now mark out your sacred space. I cannot help you with this task, for you alone can lay your frithstead's foundations."

The ground is softened by the rain and, although your work takes effort, time seems to bend and it is soon complete.

Frigg smiles, "You have wrought well! Let us bless your heart's home. For here your heritage and legacy will grow with your choices and deeds. What legacy will you build for those who come after?"

Together you galdr (chant) Othala (ᛟ) three times.

It is now time to return. Thank Frigg for her guidance and those things that are needful.

Frigg smiles, and marks your brow with Gebo (ᚷ), a gift for a gift. "I name you frithweaver. Go with my blessing." She walks across the field and vanishes in a rainbow blaze.

You return down the path, now sunlit, that you traveled to the place you know well and feel your body at rest in the here and now. Breathe deeply—in and out—wiggle your fingers and toes, stretch and when you are ready, open your eyes.

Blót to Frigg (M. Durkan)

Items: Altar, light blue or white tablecloth, flowers, blót bowl, statue or image of Frigg, two horns, bottle(s) of mead and a non-alcoholic beverage, spindle-carded wool, pieces of white wool yarn cut in 4-5 inch pieces (these are for participants, so have enough for each person).

I. Creation of Sacred Space

Gythia: (*signs Hammer—red energy*) Hammer in the North, Hallow and Hold this Holy Stead!
Folk: Hallow and hold this Holy Stead!
Gythia: Hammer in the East, hallow and hold this Holy Stead!
Folk: Hallow and hold this Holy Stead!
Gythia: Hammer in the South, hallow and hold this Holy Stead!
Folk: Hallow and hold this Holy Stead!
Gythia: Hammer in the West, hallow and hold this Holy Stead!
Folk: Hallow and hold this Holy Stead!
Gythia: Hammer over us, hallow and hold this Holy Stead!
Folk: Hallow and hold this Holy Stead!
Gythia: Hammer under us, hallow and hold this Holy Stead!
Folk: Hallow and hold this Holy Stead!
Gythia: Around us and in us Asgard and Midgard!

II. Invocation:

Gythia (*elhaz stance*): Holy one hear us and be here now!
(*Sings invocation to Frigg:* https://www.youtube.com/watch?v=bugAzHn-doKQ)

> Frigga, Frigga
> All Mother— Queen Beloved
> **Folk: We call to you**

> Frigga, Frigga
> Key Keeper, Peace-weaver
> **Folk: We call to you**

From the Marsh Hall
Folk: Come to us
From the High Seat
Folk: Come to us
From the hearth's warmth
Folk: Come to us
From the heart's core
Folk: Come to us.

Frigga Frigga
Far seeing—Wyrd Spinner
Folk: We call to you
Frigga, Frigga
Rune Warden, Secret Keeper
Folk: We call to you

From the Marsh Hall
Folk: Come to us
From the High Seat
Folk: Come to us
From the hearth's warmth
Folk: Come to us
From the heart's core

Frigga, Frigga
Homemaker—Joy of Kindred
Folk: We call to you

Frigga, Frigga
Caretaker, Wise Protectress
Folk: We call to you

From the Marsh Hall
Folk: Come to us
From the High Seat
Folk: Come to us

From the Hearth's Warmth
Folk: Come to us
From the Heart's core
Folk: Come to us
Frigga, Frigga
 All Mother— Queen Beloved
Folk: We call to you

Gythia: Beloved All-Mother, we are gathered around your altar seeking your wisdom and your blessing! Teach us the lessons of commitment and frith!
Folk: Hail Frigg!

III. Visioning

Gythia: Please take a seat or find a comfortable position to take a personal journey to Frigg—to know Her more deeply and to understand ourselves more clearly.

Gythia leads folk through the visioning: Take a deep breath in and out—and another. Release your tensions and worries of the day with each breath. Now, send a tendril of your energy into the earth, through surface soils and rocks, past deep rivers and into the earth's molten heart. Now draw a bit of that red earth energy up. Let it travel from your feet through the crown of you head filling you and grounding you to this time and place. You are relaxed and at peace. Safely you will journey and safely you will return to this place and time.

Breath in, and as you breath out, move out of your body. See a place that you know well. The sun is has just risen and just ahead is the beginnings of a path. Follow it away from this familiar place into a woodland until you come to a meadow.

In its center is Yggdrasil, Tree of the ages, Center-post of the world.

The path spirals inward. Follow it until you stand at the base of the World Tree. Reach out and touch its gnarled and rugged beauty, listen as it whispers of secrets hidden beneath its three great roots and within its weathered bark.

Now the part of the trunk closest to you begins to glow. A doorway appears and opens, and you walk into the tree. Feel the pulsing life that surrounds you. Smell the scents of earth and green things. Sense its vastness and age. An emerald light illuminates another doorway with a latch carved like a drop spindle.

You open the door and step forward and find yourself in a beautiful wetland sparking in the early morning sunlight. The path ends where swans glide on sparking water. Great blue herons with heavy wings and lazy flight flap toward a spot where fish jump.

A house sits just beyond tussocks of green marsh grass and whispering reeds. It is your heart's home. How does it appear to you?

The door opens and the All Mother stands on the threshold. She waves and calls to you. Her voice is pure and strong.

"Hail and welcome! This is a path of the heart. If you desire to come to The Marsh Hall, you will find the path."

Filled with expectation, you make your way to Her. At last, you reach the open door and Frigg bids you enter, and you thank Her. A fire burns in the hearth, and sweet-smelling herbs hang from the rafters. A great birchwood loom leans against the wall. Next to it are two chairs, a basket of wool roving as white as fair weather clouds, and a drop spindle.

Frigg sits and takes up the spindle.

"Come, sit beside me my child. Tell me why you have made this journey."

You speak to Her from the heart, holding nothing back.

(pause for participants to speak to Frigg)

When you have finished, she offers you the basket of wool roving.

"Take a piece of wool. Smell its scent, feel the fibers, yet unspun into the web of wyrd. Hold it. Bless it. Fill it with your energy and your fondest hopes, then—if you choose—give it to me."

You hand the All Mother the wool. Humming a lullaby, she hooks the wool onto the top of the spindle and holding the fleece between her thumb and index finger, pulls down and twists expertly, turning that which is becoming into that which is. Feel the power of her spinning turn within you as your hope becomes a possibility—a way forward toward your goal. When the wool is spun into a sturdy yarn, She unhooks it, ties a knot at the base and hands you the other end.

Feel Frigg's power traveling through the yarn and through the life force and energy you put into it. She smiles.

"This is a binding between us in this place and time, filled with your hope and intent, and spun into being by my hand. This is what you need to move forward—my gift to you."

For a moment, the yarn shines and you see a shape made just for you. What is it that you see?

You gaze into her eyes and perceive some of the depth of her bneing. Her eyes are clear pools that mirror your own face. She looks at you with a mother's love and says, "Take this token and use it wisely."

If you wish to say anything to Frigg or ask Her anything, you may do so at this time. If you have nothing to ask, sit and listen to anything else she might say.

(pause for participants to speak with Frigg)

After a time, Frigg says, "It is time for you to go, my child, but your return journey will be by another path."

She opens another door where a guide awaits you. Who has she summoned for you? You thank her again and follow your guide. (*pause*)

You guide touches your shoulder, Fensalir shimmers and vanishes, and you find yourself before the Rainbow Bridge. Your guide tells you that this road will take you home. You thank your guide and travel down the rainbow bridge. Now take a deep breath. Sink down into your body. Wiggle your fingers and toes. Feel your body and its connection to the earth and to this place and time. Remember what you have learned and when you are ready, open your eyes.

IV. Hallowing: Gythia Blesses Horns and Asks Frigg for Her Blessing.
Gythia lifts the horn of mead:

In the name of Frigg, All Mother, I hallow this drink, fruit of the earth,
With Gebo uniting giver, receiver, and gift in an equal exchange (galdrs Gebo)
    In the name of Frigg, All Mother, I hallow this drink with **Perthro**, the lot box and the well. Keeper of the mysteries illuminate our wyrd!
    In the name of Frigg All Mother, I hallow this drink with **Berkano,** the Birch Tree—great goddess rune of protection and renewal, Mother may you always protect us!
    In the name of Frigg, All Mother, I hallow this horn with **Othala**, holy home of kin of body and spirit. Lady of hearth and home, hold us in your keeping and keep us in your heart.

V. The Horn is Passed. Frigg is hailed.
Each person takes a drink or raises horn with reverence and offers their hail over the horn to Frigg. The remainder of the horn is poured into the Hlaut bowl.

VI. Blessing
The participants and the altar are sprinkled with the hallowed drink.

VII. Hail and Farewell

Gythia: Beloved Lady, for the gifts given we give thanks! All Hail to your
    coming! All Hail to your going!
Folk: All hail to you hence and hither! (*Vafþrúðnismál* 4)
Gythia: Now is done the holy work of word and deed.

VIII. Earth libation

Folk visualize the red hammers sinking into the ground.
Gythia: From the gods, to the earth to us. From us, to the earth, to the
    gods. A gift for a gift.
Hlautbowl is earthed.

Frigg as envisioned by John Charles Dollman,
in Sander, *Edda Sämund den Vises* (1893)

Mother's Night Blót (M Durkan)

This blót is also appropriate for Dísablót/Disting held at the beginning of February. My local folk hail Frigg and the Disir on the Anglo-Saxon *Modraniht* or "Mother's Night," which takes place just before the winter solstice. This is a beautiful way to begin the Yule season.

Items: Candle and candle holders for each participant, altar cloth, statues and/or images of the Matronae and Frigg, photos of beloved women, altar candles, flowers, objects connected to beloved women, cookies, baked goods. Horn, blót-bowl, blót tine, pen and a journal/notebook, mead and non alcoholic beverage.

I. Creation of Sacred Space

Gythia (*signs Hammer—red energy*): Hammer in the North, /Hallow and Hold this Holy Stead! (She repeats this in the East, South, West, Above, and Below.)

Alternately: Gythia traces a spiral in the air, representing a spindle, and says: In the North [East, South, West, Above Us, Below Us], All-Mother guard and guide us!

II. Invocation

All Folk: Hail mother Nerthus, Sacred Earth, you who nurture us. May you continue to uphold us. Hail mother Frigga, beloved Great Mother of hearth and home. May you keep our household whole and safe.
Hail mother Freyja, Lady of the Vanir. May we receive prosperity in the coming year. Hail to our family's Mothers, our Dísir, going back in a line to the beginning.

My blessed family matrons. Tonight, in honor of your sacrifices, that which were necessary to bring forth my family, I give praise you as we celebrate the wonders of life, and love.

Hail to the mothers who walk with us here! You who have watched over us and loved us always—the thread of whose lives are bound to ours—bless us in the coming year! We remember you with love and honor you this night.

All sing "Mother's Night" to the tune of "Silent Night" (lyrics by Maire Durkan):

Peaceful night, Mothers Night
Beloved women. Shining bright
Heartbeat to heartbeat, an unbroken song
Wisdom given and love passed on
Guide our way, help us grow
Guide our way, help us grow.

Wondrous night, Mothers Night
Seen and unseen, Guiding lights
Mortal, immortal, we honor you here
For your journeys, your laughter, your tears
Praise our blessed Disir
Praise our blessed Disir.

Silent Night Holy Night
All is calm, all is bright
Lives made beautiful through your deeds,
Hands that worked to fulfill others' needs
Mothers Dear, fill this space
And bless us all with your grace.

Gythia: And They are here! We bid you, hail and welcome!
Folk: Hail and welcome!

III. Readings and Statements of Intent

First volunteer reads:
They began the year on that very night, which we hold so sacred, which they used to call by the heathen word Mōdraniht, that is "mother's night," because of the ceremonies they enacted all that night. —*De Temporum Ratione*, the Venerable Bede

Gythia: Mōdraniht, or Mother's Night is a celebration of Frigga and the Disir, the female ancestral spirits that guide and protect the family line down through the ages. Tonight, on Solstice Eve, the first night of Yule, we honor our mortal and immortal Mothers, both those that abide with us in this world and those who have passed into the next. In modern Heathenry, and for those who follow a Northern Tradition path, Yule is a sacred between-time, when the old year dies, the new one is shaped, and the boundaries between the mundane and sacred become porous, letting both might and danger into the world. That the first night of the most potent Holy Tide of the Heathen year begins by honoring the female powers seems fitting—especially in winter, a time of physical hardship, a time of spiritual danger when "the dead walk freely, [and] trolls and alfar come into the homes of humans. . . ." and at a time of celebration of and with family and community.

Second volunteer reads:

There are a number of customs that are attributed to Mother's Night. Traditionally, at dusk, a candle is lit in the home and shines throughout the night. This light is used by the Disir to pierce the veil and watch over the family until the first light of day reaches the hearth. The ancestral disir use this night to give blessings to the family, to mothers and to mothers to be. The lighting of the candle signifies the start of Yule. At the nightly meal a place is set for the Disir so that they may join in the celebration and libations are poured in their honor. This is a night for telling stories about the female ancestors of the family and to decorate a Yule tree as decorating the home with evergreen is a traditional holiday custom.

Gythia: The deep night of the year, the dark stillness before the sun is reborn, and the eve of Balder's birth is before us. We come together in darkness to honor Mother Frigg and the Disir, and ask blessings on all mothers, or mothers yet to be.

IV. Candle Rite

Gythia lights candle from the candle on Mother's Night Altar, and says: "Now each of us, will pass the flame as each generation of mothers has passed it before us, as we name our lineage through our mothers and ancestresses of blood and spirit to the best of our ability. Be sure to include at least one generation that is deceased. Go back as many generations as you wish (within reason). After each person recites their ancestry, light the next person's candle."

[A quick note here — many people are adopted. If you are one of them, you are fortunate enough to be able to choose whether you wish to honor your adoptive family, your biological family, or a combination of the two. If you don't know the names of your birth parents or their ancestry, there's nothing wrong with saying, "Child of a family unknown." It's entirely up to you. The spirits of your ancestors know who you are, even if you don't know them yet.]

"I_____ daughter/son/child of_____ who(tell something about your mother), grandchild of _____ who (tell something if you know it) and _____(the other grandmother if you know her name). . . [etc . You may also name women who are paternal grandmothers. End with:] I honor you! May you be blessed and may you bless me and watch over my journey in this life.

V. Visioning to the Mothers

Gythia: Relax. . . take some deep cleansing breaths. . . breathe in. . . breathe out. . . breathe in. . . breathe out. . . Feel yourself connecting to the Earth below. . . feel the energy of the Earth climbing up your spine. . . and breathe in. . . breathe out. . . Feel yourself bathed in the energy of the Sun and wind. . . breathe in. . . and breathe out. . . let go of the world around you. . . be right here. . . be right now. . . you float on the wind. . . breathe in. . . breathe out. . . and as you float on the wind. . . you float downwards until you stand on a path on the border of a woods. It is Solstice eve. A cold wind sings in the treetops. Night is falling and you do not wish to be alone here outside of the innangarth. Just ahead you see a cloaked figure who carries a lantern. She pushes the hood of her cloak back and a beautiful woman, neither young nor old but with the wisdom of the ages in her eyes smiles at you.

"Welcome to your innangarth. Here your Mothers wait to feast with you. Look!"

Through the trees you see your heart's home. How does it look to you?

The beautiful woman leads you forward. "You will feel a tingling as you pass through a ward of protection made by your Disir so that only you can enter this sacred space tonight."

You hear music and laughter and through the windows you can see the flicker of lights. On the door before you is a sigil made just for you.

"Say its name," The Lady says, "and enter."

Inside is a huge round table where women sit feasting. As the Lady takes Her seat, some hail and welcome you by your name in this life and others by names from past lives. They seat you in a place of honor, and you are surrounded by their love and warmth.

Then, around the table, you see before you familiar faces and faces that seem familiar. One by one some of the women, those who you loved in this lifetime or another, some who you do not know but to whom you are connected by blood or spirit, come up to you. One by one, each woman grasps your hands. As each touches your hands, you see them clearly. . . Each woman gives the gift of a memory or message like a bright star. . . Memories of a lifetime lived. . . memories which bring you joy or sorrow.

. . the brightness of a summer's day. . . the darkness of a loss, the joy of a task well done. . . the raising of a family. . . Listen to them now.

Now the beautiful woman rises from Her chair and touches your shoulder. You know now that she is Frigg All-mother.

"It is time to return, my precious child. You will hold all that you need from this night in your heart."

You bow to these women who are your Disir. Thank them now in your own words. They call words of love to you softly as their forms and voices fade and the lights of the hall dim. . .

Now warm. . . and safe. . . you float in velvet darkness. . . surrounded by the energy of the All Mother, the beating of Her heart surrounds you. . . and you become aware of your own heart beat. . . You breathe deeply. . . and the air is clean and fresh. . . Slowly you open your eyes, and realize that you are moving through a ring of shining Othalas. And in the center of the ring a basket of shimmering threads. Frigg says, "Choose wisely. . . take with you what you need". . . and so you chose which memories to take with you into this life, and you know that only that which you chose will go with you. . . all else Frigg will purify.

Take a deep breath. And another.

As you settle back into your body, feel its weight, the energy of this place and time know that you are cleansed, know that you are safe.....and you know that you are loved..

When you are ready, open your eyes and return to this world... You may write notes in your journal if you choose, or sit quietly and reflect.

VI. Hallowing

Volunteer and Gythia hold horns. Gythia traces each rune over each horn. Gythia blesses horns with runes Berkano and Othala, and asks All Mother and Disir for their blessings.

Gythia: I sign these horns with **Berkano**—Great Goddess rune of protection.

I sign these horns with **Othala**—Sacred Hearth and heart's home of kin and ancestresses.

Mothers, may you always watch over us, and help us to be weavers of Frith within our households and communities.

The horn is passed. (Decide on the number of rounds ahead of time, so you can plan of bottle of mead needed). Each person takes a drink or raises horn, and offers their hail over the horn to Frigg and the Disir. The remainder of the horn is poured into the Hlaut bowl.

VII. Blessing

Gythia places evergreen sprig in blessing bowl and sprinkles the altar. Walking sunwise around the circle, Gythia anoints each of the celebrants with mead saying: "The blessings of Frigga and the Disir be with you."

VIII.   Hail and Farewell

Gythia: All-Mother, Joy of Kindred, Wise Protectress, we thank you for your presence here tonight.

Blessed Disir, mothers of our blood and spirit, we thank you for your presence, your guidance, your wisdom, and protection. Seen and unseen, known and those whose names are not known to us. We hold you in our hearts. All thanks to the housewights and landwights who share this space and bless us with your presence. Stay if you will or depart now in peace. The blót is now ended.

All: As You well-came to us,
We now bid you Hail and Farewell!

All sing *Merry Yule and Mothers' Night* (to the tune of *God Rest You Merry Gentlemen*):

Merry Yule and Mothers' Night,
May you be safe and warm!
May Norns and Disir lend you light
To keep you from all harm!
Midwinter tide has come, and now the year will turn again,
May the Gods bless your kith and kin and home,
Kinfolk and home,
May the Gods bless your kinfolk and your home.

Midwinter Sun shines bright at noon
In crisp and azure skies,
Midwinter night, the snow-white moon
Among the stars will rise.
In frith within and frith without we celebrate tonight,
May the Gods bless your kith and kin and home,
Kinfolk and home,
May the Gods bless your kinfolk and your home.

O may your year be ever kind,
Bring happiness and mirth,
Peace and plenty all around,
And fire in your hearth.
May Æsir, Vanir and good wights upon your journey smile,
May the Gods bless your kith and kin and home,
Kinfolk and home,
May the Gods bless your kinfolk and your home.

© Michaela Macha

IX. Earth Libation

The Folk visualize the rune hammers (or spirals) sinking into the ground. The hlautbowl is earthed.

All: From the gods to the Earth to Us. From us to the Earth to the Gods. A gift for a gift.

Healing Rite Using Runic Forces (By Kathy Wheeler)

Kathy Wheeler wrote this beautiful rite for me when I was able to handle being up after my bilateral mastectomies. In it, participants galdred and invoked Frigg, Eir, and Odin to aid in my healing. The Healing properties of the runes were instilled and bound into a fire agate in the section of the ritual that established a new pattern. As this rite involved participants from two traditions, elements of both were incorporated. This rite can be modified for anyone who needs healing.

1. Rune Ring Casting
   a. Cast the rune ring around the space.
   b. When the ring is cast, we say together:
   By these runes of blazing red
   Hallow and hold this holy stead.

2. Statement
   a. Statement should include the following sentiments:
      i. We are here to heal the healer
      ii. We are here to help the healer heal herself
      iii. The story of the journey and struggles of [*Name of person to be healed*]
      iv. Focus on the new beginning she has created by taking the steps she has chosen

3. Invocation
   a. Odin—invocation should include the following sentiments:
      i. We call to the Father that has walked all roads, when they are easy and when they are hard
      ii. We call to the Master of the runes we use in life, and for the runes we will use in this ritual of healing for [*Name*]
      iii. Guide us to use them effectively to help [*Name*] continue her healing journey
      iv. Light His candle
      v. Blessed be

b. Frigga—the invocation should include the following sentiments…
  i. We call to the Mother that cares for all mothers, when they give and give to their families and need help caring for themselves
  ii. We call to the goddess weaver, that helps us to weave our path as we make our choices, as [Name] has made her choices to be healthy
  iii. Aid us in this ritual of healing for [Name], and aid her in caring for herself, resting, healing, and recuperating
  iv. Light Her candle
  v. Blessed be

c. Eir—invocation by [Name], calling in the Norse Goddess of healing
  i. Person being healed speaks from the heart to invoke Eir to join us
  ii. Eir's candle is lit
  iii. Blessed be
d. Song "Within Every Soul"

> *God and Goddess live within every soul*
> *Blessed their gifts, Blessed are we*
> *When we call Their names, They awaken within*
> *Blessed their gifts, Blessed are we*
> —Ivo Domínguez, Jr.

4. Awakening the Healers Within
a. [Recipient of Healing] sits in the center, and she opens herself receptively to the process (hands are resting on her lap, palm up to and open to receive)
b. We awaken the healers within her lower self, her middle self, and her higher self, so all of her parts of self are aligned and prepared to accept the gifts of healing in this ritual
c. We face [Name] and extend our hands to focus gentle healing energy toward her
  i. Root chakra, while toning **URUZ**
  ii. Solar plexus chakra, while toning **URUZ**
  iii. Third eye chakra, while toning **URUZ**

5. Elemental Healing

a. [*Recipient of Healing*] sits in the chair

b. She is given the pouch with the fire agate

c. She takes the stone out of the pouch, holds it in her hand, and imprints it with her energy

d. [After this point, only the person being healed may touch the fire agate stone]

e. AIR PERSON

   i. The appointed Air person (best case Air sun sign) walks to the East gate

   ii. Sings "Air I Am" four times while pulling in Air energy to create a glowing ball of healing Air energy in between their hands

   iii. When the ball is formed and the chant is finished, the Air person carries the energy ball from East to [*Name*]

   iv. With hands cupped above [*Name*], they pour the Air healing ball onto [*Name*] and the fire agate

f. FIRE PERSON

   i. Repeats steps above for South gate ("Fire I Am")

g. WATER PERSON

   i. Repeats steps above for the West gate ("Water I Am")

h. EARTH PERSON

   i. Repeats steps above for the North gate ("Earth I Am")

i. Sealing the Elemental Healing

   i. We all turn to the center, facing [*Name*], and seal the working by visualizing [*Name*] and the fire agate glowing with healing energy while we chant **LAGUZ** three times

6. Establishing a New Pattern (*The full script for each rune is attached at the end of this rite*)

a. The pre-cut length of cord is taken from the central altar and given to Maire to hold

b. Statement:

[*Name*], you hold in your hands a length of cord. As you have woven every minute of every day of your life with love and caring and passion, may the new pattern you establish with this working be filled with joy, beauty and healing. This cord symbolizes your new beginning and a fresh start going forward. As we knot it with runes, it will capture the magick and healing of this ritual.

c. [*Person being healed*] holds the end of the cord
d. Leader takes the end of the cord and
    i. Says the name of the first rune
    ii. Galders the name of the first rune and prepares the knot
    iii. The first speaker reads the three key words off the rune card
    iv. Leader says the name of the rune again and knots the cord
    v. The first reader flips the card and passes the cards to the next reader
    vi. The process continues until all the rune knots are complete
e. When the cord is done, have Maire place the pouch with the fire agate on the cord, knot it, and put it on
f. We chant **BERKANO** three times to aid her in birthing her new future path

7. Fixing the Memory of Healing
a. [*Person being healed*] may wish to share a few words at this time
b. [*Person being healed*]drinks of the Grail of healing
c. Sing this song of healing in honor of Frigga and [*Name*]

> *As I care for them, let Her care for me*
> *As I give to them, let Her give to me*
> *As I support them, let Her cradle me*
> *As I carry on, let Her walk with me*
>   —*"The Lady's Healing Chant." Kathy W., 9/11/18*

8. Offering Thanks
a. Thanks are offered to Lady Eir for Her healing presence and support
b. Thanks are offered to Lady Frigga for Her presence and support
c. Thanks are offered to Lord Odin for His presence and support
d. We bid them hail and farewell
e. Candles are blown out

9. Rune Ring Dismissal
a. Leader dismisses the rune ring

10. Circle Dismissal
a. Second Leader uses the Grail, to close the circle using invoking Earth pentacles in each quarter

b. **Merry meet. Merry part. And Merry meet again.**

Items Needed: Quarter and central altar tables
    White altar cloths
    Odin statue
    Frigga statue
    Eir statue (corn dolly)
    Grail
    Comfortable chair in center for person being healed

Additional Supplies:
    Tattva altar cloths
    Tattva candles and candle holders
    Lighter
    3 taper candles in holders
    Cord
    Pouch
    Fire Agate
    Rune cards (Key Words)

    Salt water purification (FM water/kosher salt)
    Incense (Ansuz incense and supplies)

To be read during the "Establishing a New Pattern" section in the ritual:
    [*Person to be healed*], may the runes bring you...
    ᚠ Fehu Prosperity of Healing
    ᚢ Uruz Reservoir of Healing
    ᚦ Thurisaz Regeneration through Healing
    ᚨ Ansuz Breath of Healing

ᚱ Raidho Journey of Healing
ᚲ Kenaz Forge of Healing
ᚷ Gebo Exchange of Healing
ᚹ Wunjo Joy through Healing
ᚺ Hagalaz Framework of Healing
ᚾ Naudhiz Persistence in Healing
ᛁ Isa Patience in Healing
ᛃ Jera Pattern of Healing
ᛇ Eihwaz Endurance of Healing
ᛈ Perthro Becoming through Healing
ᛉ Elhaz Protection in Healing
ᛊ Sowilo Brilliance in Healing
ᛏ Tiwaz Victory in Healing
ᛒ Berkano Evolution in Healing
ᛖ Ehwaz Harmony through Healing
ᛗ Mannaz Community of Healing
ᛚ Laguz Current of Healing
ᛜ Ingwaz Potential in Healing
ᛞ Dagaz Synthesis of Healing
ᛟ Othala Inheritance of Healing

Woman / Adult Making Rite (written by M. Durkan)

Preparations: *This rite can be amended to be non-gender specific/binary]. My daughter wanted to be surrounded by the women she knows and loves, who invoked the power of the Divine Feminine, which resides within all beings. Everyone should think of what blessing and advice they'd want to give and how they will talk about the beauty and might of the changes her body is undergoing.*

Items: Toy or doll symbolizing my daughter's childhood, for her to place on the altar. Spindle with wool to be drawn; red roses; token from Crone (amulet, crystal). Altar to goddess as maiden [Idunna or Ostara], mother [Frigg], and crone [Frau Holle/Mother Hulda]. My daughter will purify in a ritual bath prior to the rite and dress in a white dress with the help of her mother who will help dress her and brush her hair. Moon time goddess altar with red roses.

I. Alignment of the Energies

We are led to ground and center calling in Root Chakra Energy in preparation for the ritual.

II. Processional and Purification

Salt water and appropriate incense. We chant "Connected, Whole, Complete" *until all are in circle, then bring in my daughter.*

III. Creation of Sacred Space

The quarters are called, and the circle is cast, calling in elements as they reflect the maiden's transition to womanhood. [For a Heathen-style ceremony, the space may be warded with Elhaz rune through galdr, hallowed with fire (candle) or with the Hammer Hallowing, or hallowed with another appropriate invocation to a deity.]

IV. Statement of Intent: The Purpose of This Ritual is Offered.

We gather to celebrate the beauty, power, and wisdom that transforms this girl into a woman and for this maiden to accept her worth as a woman. Our blood is a sacred source— the Great Mother's gift passed from generation to generation. When the time is right, moon magic works within us and we must bleed. This is the power of the goddess connecting us to our deepest truth. This is who you are—who we are. And in the blessing and gift we are connect, whole, and complete. Blessed be!

V. Maiden, Mother, Crone Impart Their Wisdom

The Maiden (*holding one of my daughter's dolls, approaches daughter, wearing light green or white, as Ostara or Idunna*):

I am The Maiden. I too have played with dolls and am full of the fire, hopes and dreams of every young woman. Yet, although a time for play never ceases, I am no longer a child. (*Passes Colleen's doll to her.*) As a symbol of this passage, are you ready to place this beloved doll upon my altar?

Daughter: Yes.

Maiden: Then say this after me. (*break up appropriately or have a script for Colleen to read*) "I release all that holds me back so that my true self can shine."

Daughter repeats: "I release all that holds me back so that my true self can shine."

All sing: She changes everything she touches
And everything she touches changes (*repeat 2 times*)

Maiden: It is done. It is time to meet the Mother. (*Maiden leads Colleen to Mother.*)

Mother (Frigg—dressed in Red for this rite unless you want to keep the light blue associated with Frigg): *Speaks to Colleen about how moon-blood has made her a woman and of what mysteries and magic are open to her now.* I am the Mother. I give you the gifts that I have. To embrace the cycles of your body and delight in its beauty and power. You have the power of creation within you! To nurture and delight in growth, to tend and to protect, to delight in the bonds of family and friends, and, yes, to let our children find their own paths as will you. *She gives daughter a token (a red rose).*

Daughter (*lays it on the altar and says*): I embrace the flow of my life and its blessings.

Mother: It is done. It is time to meet the Wise Woman who we call the Crone. *Maiden leads Daughter to Crone.*

All sing: She changes everything she touches
And everything she touches changes (repeat 2 times)

Crone [Holde/Frau Holle}: I am the Crone. I give you the gift of sacrifice. Moon time means honoring and learning from the whole process including the aches and pains that may be part of your moon time.

(*Crone will speak of the wisdom and lessons of womanhood beyond blood and children. Crone gives Colleen a token: an amulet, stone, crystal*) Take this token to remind you of this time and to carry with you on your journey.

Daughter: (*places token on the altar and repeats after Crone:*) I am whole. I am loved. I give thanks for all that I am and all that I will be.

All sing: She changes everything she touches
And everything she touches changes (*repeat 2 times*)
[https://www.youtube.com/watch?v=nVwF34LcZCg]

VI: Blessings and Cord Cutting

Each woman in the group will pull and spin a bit of yarn on the spindle, then share some wisdom, speak of the goddess they follow and impart a blessing for the Daughter, then pass the spindle. When this is done the spindle is presented to the Daughter, who can pull and spin a bit and name her hopes if she chooses. She will then lay the pulled yarn on the altar for the God-desses' blessing.

All: You now stand as a full-grown woman in the company of the ances-tresses[Disir], goddesses, and your sisters here on earth! Blessed Be!
(*For Heathen rites a faining or sumbel—with non-alcoholic beverage—can be added here*)

VII. Cakes and Ale

Cakes and ale are blessed by the young adult and her parent or sponsor. The young adult and their sponsor carry them to everyone.

VIII. Thanks and Release

The holy beings and wights are thanked for their presence.
All: All hail to your coming
All Hail to your going
Hail !

Of course, honor Frigg as often as you can (I honor her daily). These are suggestions and the dates that I use for larger gatherings or more formal rites. The dates that you celebrate may differ from mine or you may celebrate other holy tides.

- Distaff Day: January 7. Blót to Frigg as patroness of craftspeople especially spinning and weaving and as a spinner of wyrd.
- Disting: Early February—another time to honor Disir. This tradition is Scandinavian.
- Walpurgisnacht: April 30/ May 1. Blót to Frigg as Lady of hearth magic.
- Mother's Day: Whenever you celebrate in your country.
- Midsummer: June 20/Summer Solstice. Honor the Lady of bounty. Ask for a successful harvest season.
- Hlafmæst/Lammas: end of July/early August. This is the first harvest festival. Thanks for bounty and prayers for continued bounty.
- Winter Nights: October 31-November 2. This feast is for the ancestors—male and female. Honor Frigg as our ancestress of spirit.
- Mother's Night: Dec 20/21. On the eve of the winter solstice, honor Frigg and mothers, living and passed, in our family lines. This tradition is Anglo-Saxon. Blót to Frigg as an ancestress and First Lady of the Disir.
- Twelve days of Yule: Winter Solstice to, approximately, January 6. The barrier between the worlds is thin. Wights of weal and bane can cross over. Ask Frigg's protection and blessings. Ask to be a frithweaver and good host as folk are welcomed into your home.

Chapter 6: Frigg's Handmaidens

Whether you consider Frigg's handmaidens to be hypostases (real and distinct beings emanating from Frigg's essence and reflecting and acting upon specific aspects of her character), or whether you see them as entirely separate goddesses, the handmaidens are part of Frigg's team and on her Board of Directors, so to speak. Each has a particular mission, department, and energy that expresses unique areas of Frigg's agenda as CEO and Asgard's queen. Interactions with each of the handmaidens helps us to call upon and connect to a specific energy, an area of expertise, we seek. Understanding and working with Frigg's handmaidens also deepens our connection to Frigg and helps us experience her energies more deeply.

Saga—The Storyteller

Saga's name is linked to the ON word *segja* which means "say" or "tell" (Simek 2007, p. 274). In Snorri's *Gylfaginning* (The Deluding of Gylfi), verse 35 lists Saga as the second goddess after Frigg (Byock 2005, p. 42). Her hall is Sokkvabekk, which can be translated as "sunken bank" or "treasure bank" (Simek 2007, p. 297). Verse 7 of the *Poetic Edda*'s *Grímnismál* (Grimnir's Sayings) states that "cool waves resound" over this hall, and that "There Odin and Saga drink every day, joyful from golden cups." (Larrington 2014, p. 49). Her sunken hall has similarities to Fensalir and Odin spends a great deal of time there, but I do not experience Saga as being Frigg per se, any more than I experience Hlín, despite the fact that Frigg is called Hlín in a kenning, as being Frigg per se. I have connected to Saga through my writing, and she is a great patroness for those who work with the spoken and written word: genealogists, historians, skalds, poets, researchers, librarians and story-tellers, to name a few. I have found her to be quite friendly with sparking good will and a droll humor, especially to those who honor their ancestors and seek to record and pass on their stories.

Hail Saga! Sage Shope!
Guardian and Gatherer,

Please share the treasure of your wisdom.
Teach us the art of storytelling
That we will not lose our heritage
Send your wisdom forth and forward
　—gift for gift—
We will tell you tales of our travels, tests, trial, and triumphs!
Help us to find the words and resources to preserve and pass on
Priceless memories,
Stories of our families and of our folk.
May we celebrate the memories of their deeds,
Their wit and wisdom.
Help us to recall, record, and forge a link
Generation to generation
So that they and we are not forgotten.
　　　—Maire Durkan

Symbols: Ink and parchment, mead cup.

Runes: Ansuz, ᚠ (the power of the spoken word); Othala, ᚷ (keeping the memory of the ancestors).

Eir—The Healer

I developed my close relationship with Eir when I found out that, like my mother who died from breast cancer when I was 14, I had inherited the breast cancer gene, BRCA I. At the time, our youngest was just turning 13. I knew what is was to lose a mother early and, if I could prevent it, I wanted to do all that I could to make sure that my risk of breast cancer was lowered appreciably. I turned to All-Mother Frigg—who informed me that I could look at this as a gift (the gift of a longer life) for a gift (giving up body parts as Odin gave up his eye to Mimir's Well or hung from Yggdrasil to gain wisdom of the runes). For the sake of my family as well as my desire to spend as much time on the planet as I could with them, I opted for bilateral mastectomies. It was soon after my first surgery that Frigg introduced me to Eir, and we have had a close relationship ever since. Eir's powers extend from Frigg's, but are specifically focused on healing.

In chapter 35 of the *Prose Edda*'s *Gylfaginning,* Eir is listed third (after Saga) and is called "the best of doctors." In *Fjölsvinnsmál* 38, she is also listed as one of Menglod's maids who sit on Lyfjaberg (ON for "healing mountain")—where all the sick and lame could find healing (Simek 198). Her name is a cognate of the Norse words for "peace; clemency" (Lindow 2002, p. 105) or "help; mercy" (Orchard 1997, p. 36).

As a witch in a healing coven and a dedicated healer who studies herb craft, it's a wonder that I didn't come to Eir sooner. But now that I have worked with her and aspected (a form of drawing down or deity possession) her for some time, I cannot imagine not having her guidance. When I was sufficiently healed, my friend Kathy Wheeler wrote a healing rite for me in which we invoked Frigg, Eir, and Odin and used the runic forces to augment healing. I felt her presence and it was one of the most powerful healing rites I had ever experienced. It can be found in the ritual section of this devotional. I find her to be calm, clear-headed, precise, practical, inquisitive, and compassionate.

> Hail Eir!
> Wise and compassionate Healer,
> May I journey often to the Hill of Healing
> May I have the perseverance, patience, and endurance
> I need to heal.
> Hear me when I call to you!
> Touch me with your healing might when I reach for you!
> Great surgeon,
> Help me to clearly see
> And remove that which does not serve my well-being.
> Help me to heal my wounds of body, mind, and spirit!
> When others reach out to me
> May I know in what ways I can best support their healing.
> Within my home and within and between my communities,
> May my words and deeds promote healing
> May the orlog that I lay down
> Build frith and healing.
> Great Healer,
> May doctors, scientists, veterinarians, researchers, nurses, counsel
>   ors, and all healers

Continue to discover the best means of healing their patients!
Help all folk to find meaningful ways to heal the hurts
And ease the pain of our wounded world,
Honoring always its wights of earth, air and water.
May I not despair in damage done.
Move and motivate me to heal what I can
And may my words and deeds
Bring balm and blessing
Like the dew-touched grass of the Hill of Healing.
      —Maire Durkan

Symbols: The mortar and pestle, healing herbs.

Runes: Berkano, ᛒ and Laguz, ᛚ (for healing); Mannaz, ᛗ (for healthy connections); Uruz, ᚢ (for primal life force).

Gefjun—The Giver

Gefjon, dragged from Gylfi
Gladly, the land beyond value,
Denmark's increase,
Steam rising from the swift-footed bulls.
The oxen bore eight
moons of the forehead and four heads,
Hauling as they went in front of
The grassy isle's wide fissure
      —Snorri Sturluson, quoting Bragi the Old
        Gylfagynning 1 and *Heimskringla, Ynglinga saga* ch. 5; Byock
        translation

In Langelinie Park in Copenhagen, Denmark there is a beautiful fountain with a monumental statue of the goddess Gefjon pushing a plough attached to four straining oxen, her Jotun sons conceived and transformed for this task. Gefjun's name means "the giving one" (Simek 2007, p. 102).

She holds the energy of Gebo—a gift for a gift in a balanced exchange that involves both an act of generosity and of sacrifice. That energy is still very much a part of who she is. Even today, Heathen and non-Heathen folk visit her fountain, toss in a coin, and make a wish (it's said it will come true).

Gefion is the only one of Frigg's handmaidens with stories as well as references in the lore (including a poem describing art on a shield). Like Saga, she has strong ties to Odin as well as to Frigg. Although there is an opinion that she is of giant stock, no sources actually state that she is a jotynja, except perhaps *Völsa þáttr*, in which a maiden calls upon her and then upon a giantess. She's never mentioned as a Jotun bride, and in Snorri's accounts she is a member of the tribe of the Æsir. While she mates with a giant, as did Loki's mother Laufey, she is never affiliated with the Jotuns (as Skadi clearly is), and is named a goddess of the Æsir on several occasions. What follows is a tale of ambition, desire, Odinic level hoodwinking, possible sexploitation, and the establishment of a kingdom and dynasty through kinship ties with Odin. What I want to establish straight off the bat is that Gefion is much more than just a minor fertility goddess and lighthearted giver of gifts.

Given the lore and my personal experiences, she is connected to agriculture, the empowerment of young women, the plough (breaking new ground both literal and metaphorical), prosperity, astute planning, material wealth based on wise management and planning (in business this includes selling yourself to customers). She's a heavyweight power who has worked very hard for the things she attained and, if you call upon her, she will expect you to put an effort into your aspirations as well!

In the *Prose Edda's Gylfagynning* 1 and in *Heimskringla's* euhemerized account in *Ynglinga saga 5,* Snorri Sturluson relates that King Gylfi of Sweden offers this "travelling woman" of the Æsir as much land as she could plough in twenty-four hours in exchange for "the pleasure of her company." (Byock, p. 9) A gift for a gift! Ah, but what the soon to be deluded king doesn't realize is that this is a goddess on a mission, whom "Odin sent north-east over the sound to look for land." She is determined. She has a goal and she is willing to give the gift of her body and of her womb to get it. She proceeds to travel to Jotunheim where she has sex with a Jotun, has four sons, shapes them in the likeness of oxen (do you think she's turned them back?), yokes them to a plough and "broke up the land unto the sea westward opposite Odensö [Odin's island]; it was called Selund [the old name for Zealand in Denmark] and there she dwelt." (*Ynglinga saga* 5, Monsen/Smith translation) Gefjon's connection to Odin continues; she marries Odin's son Skjold [a.k.a. Beowulf's Scyld Sceafing] and they make their home on the island near where all Danish kings have been buried. Like Odin's Gangleri or Grimnir, Gefjon disguises herself and uses her sexual prowess to get what she wants.

Her links to Odin as a seer, traveler, and founder of dynasties are further stressed when Odin defends her against Loki's accusations in the *Poetic Edda*'s *Lokasenna*. She acts as a frithweaver (no surprise, as she is a member of Frigg's team) and attempts to ease Loki's war of words by giving good counsel:

> "Why would you two Æsir in here
> Fight with wounding words?
> Isn't it known of Loki that he likes a joke
> And all the gods love him?" (Larrington, p. 84)

Not being the least bit interested in frith, Loki then tells her to "shut up" and accuses her of wrapping her thighs around "the white boy" (possibly Gylfi or Heimdall) for a piece of jewelry. It is interesting that it is Odin himself who defends her as a goddess worthy of respect in her own right and an embodiment of Frigg's might who shares Frigg's power of foresight:

> Mad you are, Loki, and out of your wits,
> When you make Gefion angry with you,
> For I think she knows all the fate of the world,
> As clearly as I do myself. (Larrington, p. 84)

Coming from Odin, those are some respectable credentials! Besides, no one really seems to care much about her sexual exploits.

Now, back to Snorri who really muddies the waters in *Gylfaginning*'s Chapter 35, where he tells us that Gefjun is the fourth goddess, that she is a maiden, and that "women who die as virgins serve her" (Byock 2005, p. 42). The only way that I can wrap my head around this is to assume is that the term "maiden" is used loosely and, although she is associated with virgins, may have less to do with actual virginity and more to do with her youthful, maidenly appearance. *Mær*, the Old Norse word for maiden, can mean daughter or wife, and "there is no evidence that the Norse placed a special value on virginity" (*Our Troth* vol. I, p. 343). I still hold that Gefjon is a sponsor and protectress of young women, especially those who are teenagers, regardless of their sexual experience, and welcomes them into her hall.

That Gefjon is associated with fertility and sexuality (or the potential fertility of a young woman) is underscored by this tidbit from *Völsa þáttr* ("Tale of the Penis"), a short story in the *Flateyjarbók,* where it is found in a chapter of *Óláfs saga helga.* The folk of a family are passing around a stallion's preserved penis in ritual, and the maiden of the home says:

> I swear by Gefjun
> and the other gods
> that against my will
> do I touch this red proboscis.
> May giantesses
> accept this holy object,
> but now, slave of my parents,
> grab hold of Völsi.

> I raise a horn to Gefjon!
> Great and wise Giver,
> May I know the power of Gebo
> The balance of gift and gift
> Sacrifice and sacrifice
> In even exchange.
> Undaunted One!
> You who stopped at nothing to achieve your desire,
> Help me to achieve my goals!
> May I plough the fields of circumstance
> Forming what I need and desire with
> Perseverance, foresight, and courage.
> Let me not be dismayed by the hardship before me

May others gift me with their support
And may I give them a gift of equal value in return.
Spur me on to use both wits and will to achieve my purpose.
Lady of Frigg's Court,
May I construct islands of frith and wellbeing
Where gifts of friendship and love are exchanged.
Help me to plan well and work hard
To achieve my dreams!
—Maire Durkan

Symbol: A plough.

Runes: Gebo, ᚷ (a gift for a gift); Uruz, ᚢ (she has primal strength and sons whom she turned into bulls); Naudhiz, ᚾ (she worked hard and toiled for what she needed); Fehu, ᚠ (wealth and good fortune).

Fulla—Keeper of Frigg's Treasures, Secrets, and Women's Mysteries

When I was a girl, I had a music box (with a spinning ballerina to boot) in which I stored my jewelry and precious keepsakes and a diary in which I wrote my most personal thoughts. Although I would share confidences with my sister and circle of female friends, and make gifts of some things from the box, I would never have dreamed of sharing *all* of the contents of my diary or my box of precious mementoes with them. Yet, Allmother Frigg does this with her "sister" goddess Fulla—so great is their love and trust— that secrets, confidences, and all of Frigg's tangible and intangible treasures (blessings, gifts of fruitfulness and prosperity in body and spirit) are in Fulla's keeping. Their relationship is one of perfect frithfulness. Fulla is a goddess who endorses and appreciates a gratitude attitude and doesn't appreciate undue whinging and whining. She has taught me that, while we live, there is always something to treasure and something for which we can be grateful and that it is our responsibility to be good custodians of what we have received.

As the goddess with whom Frigg shares her secrets, the goddess listed as Frigg's sister (and fellow healer) in the Second Merseburg Charm, and as the one who shares a close and intimate relationship with Frigg, Fulla is connected to the bonds of friendship, love, and trust between women. Baldr's wife Nanna sends back gifts for both Frigg and Fulla, which indicates her status among the ásynjur. In chapter 35 of *Gylfaginning*, Snorri sates that she is a virgin with long, flowing unbound hair and wears a gold band around her head. Fulla carries Frigg's treasure box, looks after her shoes, and shares Frigg's secrets. In Snorri's *Skáldskaparmál*, "the headband of Fulla" is listed as a kenning for gold (Byock 2005, p. 114). As a sharer of Frigg's secrets and her "sister," Fulla acts as Frigg's close counselor. As her name can be translated as "full," Fulla is a goddess of hidden treasure and abundance. Her name may be related to the Old Norse word for cup which is also the term for a blót or ritual cup. And as the one responsible for Frigg's jewels, she is also connected to the wealth of blessings that Frigg dispenses. This relationship between the Allmother and Fulla demonstrates a huge degree of love and trust and is the epitome of a frithful relationship. So great is the trust shared between them that in *Grímnismál*, when Frigg and Odin fostered two royal brothers, and Odin counseled his foster son to betray his brother and set him adrift at sea, Frigg sends Fulla to warn King Geirod that a powerful wizard (Odin in disguise) is on his way, and that the king should be on his guard.

In my encounters with her, Fulla is cheerful, brisk, personable, and observant. One way to connect more deeply with Fulla is to make or purchase a box (these are available at arts and crafts stores), decorate it as you see fit (perhaps adding the rune Fehu, ᚠ, for prosperity and Berkano, ᛒ, for the divine feminine). Place your chest on an altar dedicated to Fulla. Write things that you treasure (objects, words that were like gifts, deeds that blessed you) on separate slips of paper as they come to you (you can always add things to your treasure chest). Ask her to bless your treasure and help you find abundance. Make another list of gifts that you may need from Fulla and the Allmother and place this beneath the chest. You can use all or part of the following invocation or make one of your own.

> Hail Fulla!
> Frigg's counselor and good sister!
> You who are entrusted with Frigg's hidden treasure
> Help me to be a good and loyal friend
> May words spoken to me and material things entrusted to me be
>   well kept.

Bestower of blessings and abundance,
Help me to recognize the blessings and abundance in my life
and to manage the elements of my life with a right good will.
Help me to find the hidden treasure within my being
Let me not be like Fafnir, a hoarder of my treasure,
But help me to be a good steward of my assets
 conserving, spending, and gifting wisely
So that the treasures of my heart and spirit increase.
Grant me the discipline needed to discover treasures, seen and
    unseen, that will enrich my life.
Keeper of Mysteries,
Help me to fare into the world of my soul and spirit
Searching the darkness as well as the light
That I may know the secrets and mysteries within.

Wake me up to the Sacred Feminine within me
As it is within all beings.
Help me to honor the presence of Allmother Frigg
And the Ásynjur, and Disir, and all Holy Female Wights
In my body
In my soul
In the sacred Earth upon which I walk
And in the very air I breathe.
Treasure keeper,
Allmother's dearest Lady,
I acknowledge the living transformative treasure of
The Sacred Feminine.
I long to reconnect my body, my soul, and my life
With the power and wisdom in your keeping.
I acknowledged that the threads and rhythms of my life and all
    lives are interconnected on the treasure box that is Midgard.
May I treasure my female friends, the sisters of my heart.
Give me courage to guard and defend the sacredness of women of
    all cultures!
Foresighted One,
Call forth in me the deep knowing not found in books
Nourish me with an abundance of wisdom and compassion

That my words and deeds are as jewels
That my legacy will be treasured.
—Maire Durkan

Symbol: Gold headband, jewelry box.

Runes: Wunjo, ᛈ (joy); Fehu, ᚠ (plenty, prosperity); Berkano, ᛒ (Goddess rune for feminine mysteries); Gebo, ᚷ (gift).

Sjöfn—Patroness of Affection, Love, and Friendship

There's no secular holiday that I love more than Thanksgiving. It's a time when we donate more to food banks, volunteer at shelters, and participate in a meal that celebrates gratitude and the affection and bonds between family and friends. It's about sharing a meal in frith (the active promotion of loyalty, love, and right good will) and fellowship. I love cooking the meal and having family members bring a dish they prepared. Most of all, I find great joy in this holiday's priceless gifts of goodwill and affection. This is the energy Sjöfn generates. Although many of Frigg's handmaiden's work with some aspect of frith, it is Sjöfn who inspires affection and friendship not only between partners, but between family members, friends, and even between humans and our fur babies. She is Frigg's designated frithweaver who inspires us to actively form and strengthen bonds of love, loyalty, and good will.

Unlike Freyja, who is associated with sexual love, in *Gylfaginning* Sjofn is listed seventh, where Snorri relates that she " is deeply committed to turning the thoughts of both men and women to love"(Byock, p. 43). Snorri states that the word for love, *sjafni*, is derived from her name. Lindow (2002, p. 268) affirms that Sjöfn is a goddess of affection and her name is used as the base for three kennings for women. Simek states that her name derives from *sefi* "sense or relation"; she is a goddess of "marriage and love, or else one of relationships"(Simek 2007, p. 286).

Alice Karlsdóttir notes that:

When the *Gylfaginning* states that Sjofn turns peoples' minds to love, the actual word used for "mind" is *hugr*, which is a broader term encompassing consciousness, intuition, and emotions as well as the intellectual process. Sjofn's power does not merely create a passing infatuation; it affects a person at the deepest level of being, touching all facets of the soul. (Karlsdóttir 2015, pp. 153-154)

My experience of Sjofn is that she promotes and encourages bonds of affection and love between partners, families, friends, and even between the seen and unseen wights (such as pets and house wights) to which one is connected. I honor her and call upon her as frithweaver and peacemaker to strengthen the bonds of affection not only between lovers/partners, but also between parents, grandparents, close friends, and even between humans and their pets. Sjöfn is a frithmaker who calls in the powers of affection to make peace and strengthen bonds. Sjöfn inspires tenderness and care and helps us manifest endearing and frithful behavior. We honor Sjöfn when we give our loved one our full attention, anticipate their needs, give hugs and words of encouragement, pay attention to little things that add up, and let them know their worth.

Question: What are some ways that you show affection?

Hail Sjöfn!
Lady of joy
May loving bonds of affection blossom
Between kith, kin, friends,
And those who will become my friends and loved ones.
Turn my thoughts toward love.
Help me to perceive
And to truly appreciate
Those most dear to me.
Through word and deed,
May I strengthen those loving bonds.
Frithweaver,
In a world filled with division and distrust
May I weave love and frith into the framework
Of my relationships
Like blended notes that form a harmony.
—Maire Durkan

Symbol: rose quartz heart, infinity knot.

Rune: Wunjo, ᛈ (joy); Othala, ᛟ (family and friendship ties); Mannaz, ᛗ (attitude towards others and to relationships).

Lofn—Permission or Blessing of Forbidden Love

In the 1950s, my aunt, from a large Roman Catholic family, met my uncle, from rock-ribbed Presbyterian stock, and they fell deeply in love. His parents did not encourage their marriage. They told my uncle that "there are enough Catholics for Catholics and enough Protestants for Protestants!" Although they had to fight for their right to be together, they got married, had two children, and lived to celebrate their fiftieth anniversary and beyond. Today, differences in religion, race, and sexual orientation still create disapproval, harassment and censure. Amnesty International states that same-sex sexual activity is a crime in seventy countries and incurs the death penalty in nine (https://www.amnesty.org/en/what-we-do/discrimination/lgbt-rights/). Also, issues concerning finances, distance, or health might pose obstacles which must be overcome. Lofn is the goddess whom Frigg has commissioned with the task of finding a way for love to triumph. If you call upon her, she will help find a way for permission to be granted.

Lofn, translated as "loving" or "permission" (Byock) and "the comforter" and "the mild" (Simek) is the eighth goddess named in Snorri's list in *Gylfaginning* 35, where he states that: "She is so gentle and so good to invoke that she has permission from All-Father or Frigg to arrange unions between men and women, even if earlier offers have been banned. From her name come the word *lof*, meaning permission as well as high praise" (Byock 2005, p. 43).

> Dearest Lofn
> Lady of Hope, Comfort, and Permission
> Guide us through the briars and snares
> That entangle us and keep us apart.
> Comforter and protector
> Let us not despair.

Open our hearts to hope
And change the minds and hearts of our leaders
May our laws protect all people's rights
May we build an accepting society
Give us the perseverance and courage
To find and create a bower
where my beloved and I can love each other freely
Lady of the keys
Open the way for us!
                    —Maire Durkan

Symbol: Keys.

Runes: Naudhiz, ᚾ (resistance leading to strength); Tiwaz, ᛏ (willingness to sacrifice for victory); Sowilo, ᛋ (success, gods honored, victory as wholeness).

Vár (Vow-er)—The One who Hears Oaths or Wards

I've included the pronunciation so that Vár's connection to oaths is clear.

> What is an Oath? In ancient and modern Heathen belief, a true oath is a statement whose implications and essence have actually been laid in the Well of Wyrd, becoming an integral part of orlay or orlog [primal layer/law]. The true oath becomes part of the pattern of That-Which-Is thus gaining the power to shape That-Which-Is-Becoming and That-Which-Should-Be, the respective domains of the three Wyrdae or Norns . By laying the oath in the Well, the deed or deeds done in fulfillment of one's oath should also fall into the Well and become part of orlay. In this way, one ensures that one's life has meaning and significance, that one's deeds—even if later forgotten by the folk—nevertheless form a permanent part of the fabric of reality.
> —Winifred Hodge, "Oaths: What They Mean and Why They Matter" *Idunna* #100, May 2015.

A memo from Vár (Oath Warden & Debt-collector)
To: Impossible, Maddening, and Dearest Children of Midgard
Re: Oaths and Their Consequences

Every day for ages beyond count, I have listened to your oaths and vows—often spoken with the greatest sincerity and a firm resolve to uphold what is sworn, but all too often with cynicism and wavering. How it irks me! How I weary of falsehoods and excuses! Do not for a moment believe that there are not consequences to your deeds and actions! Even in a world where people feel the old saying, "My word is my bond," is naïve, an oath is a weighty matter. Like a planet that creates a curvature in space-time, our sworn oaths are set into the Well and affect the Web of Wyrd. Nevertheless, whether it is a marriage oath, a presidential oath, an oath before a judge, or an oath sworn before any group, you humans still believe in the power of oaths and know that that power has consequences. Our oaths are serious, sacred business. Rest assured that I preside over each and every one. Never make an oath that you fear you cannot fulfill! Yet even the gods have had to break oaths (with consequences). Sometimes oaths conflict, or circumstances and responsibilities change, and we cannot uphold an oath. But there is a consequence for us, for the person to whom or for whom the oath was sworn, and for those who witnessed the oath. For this reason, I demand that the oath-breaker name and pay shild—an agreed upon debt—to the hearer and even to the community should you be unable to keep your oath. The shild should be no less weighty than your oath—all deeds have consequences. Before all else, strive to uphold your oaths, but find an honorable means of release from your oaths and vows if you absolutely must. Whether your oath is upheld or released, know that I witness and watch. Know that I ward your vows and hold you to honor your debts!

Sincerely
Vár
Circle of Frith
Fensalir, Asgard

According to Snorri, Vár, the ninth goddess listed, "listens to the oaths and private agreements that are made between men and women. For this reason such agreements are called *várar*. She takes vengeance on those who break trust" (Byock 2005 43).

Her name means "beloved" in Old Norse and may be linked to the term *várda* meaning guarantee, and to *varðlokkur*—a song of protection.

(*Our Troth*, vol. I, p. 347). My experience of Vár is that she is intense, sincere, watchful, and wise. Like Tyr, she will hold you to your vows and expect proper compensation should you need to be released from them.

> Hail Var
> Wise Witness
> May I hold my vows sacred
> Grant me the honor and strength
> To be true to my promises
> May my words and deeds bring me honor
> Lady of the Oath Ring,
> Illuminate my deliberations
> That I may make the right choice
> Even if that choice is hard
> And the consequences difficult
> May I speak no oaths or promises in haste
> For my sake and the sake of my community.
> —Maire Durkan

Symbol: Oath Ring.

Runes: Mannaz, ᛘ (human relationships); Ehwaz, ᛗ (trust, loyalty, teamwork); Kenaz, ᚲ (vision, harnessed power); Tiwaz, ᛏ (justice).

Vor—Lady of Awareness

As a witch and a gythia, Vor is a goddess I call upon for guidance in the realm for divination, insight and foresight. As Frigg's designated seeress, she guides me in the dream and astral realms. I have aspected (a form of deity possession) Vor and have found her to be calm, centered, perceptive, and observant. Her speech is considered and measured. When she speaks, she is perceiving what is, is becoming, and what should be, and unlike Frigg (and with her permission) will speak of choices and their consequences.

Tenth in the list of goddesses, Snorri says of Vor, "the careful one," that she is "so knowledgeable and inquires so deeply that nothing can be hidden from her. Hence the expression that a woman becomes aware '*vor*' of what she learns" (Byock 2005, p. 43). If you consult the runes, scry, or use other tools of divination, call upon her for discernment of the meaning and an accurate expression of the message. She helps us become aware of and intuit wisdom beyond what is superficially apparent. She is a guide to our parts of self, and she will be our guide into the spirit realm so that that we may come to know ourselves better. She helps us with our shadow work when we look and journey within to see what is hidden. She is the feeling that one path is more beneficial than another, the prickle on the back of your neck that warns you away from a certain turn in the road, the image or words that arise when you cast the runes or scry.

> Hail Vor!
> Wise Seeress
> Gentle Guide
> Join me on my journey
> I welcome your guidance!
> As I fare beyond,
> Help me draw forth hidden wisdom
> From the well of spirit.
> For the benefit of the seen and unseen
> Help me to divine what is needed,
> When I cast the runes, speak my visions,
> Or fare beyond the veil.
> —Maire Durkan

Symbol: A veil, a scrying bowl.

Runes: Perthro, ⌈ (the Well of Wyrd, hidden things and occult abilities); Kenaz, ⟨ (revelation); Raidho, ℝ (seeing a larger perspective, journeys); Eiwaz, ʃ (connection and communication between realms).

Syn—Guardian of Doors, Keeper of Boundaries (The Defense)

In the Harry Potter series, the battle scarred former auror (aka a warrior witch who battles the dark arts) Alastor "Mad-Eye" Moody's tagline is "constant vigilance!" "Constant vigilance" is a term we can apply to Syn as well. As Heimdall guards Asgard from the Bifrost, Syn guards the doors and boundaries of Fensalir. But Frigg's realm extends to each of us who are her children in Midgard and Syn guards our boundaries, seen and unseen, against baneful, unwanted encroachments.

Her name means refusal/denial and Snorri tell us that Syn, guards the doors of Frigg's hall and bars entry to those who are uninvited. Like Tyr, Syn is connected to legal justice as Frigg appointed her to, "defend cases she wants to see refuted in the courts. From this situation comes the expression that a denial (*syn*) is advanced when something is refused" (Byock 2005 43). This aspect of Syn's sphere of influence also demonstrates that Frigg has a keen interest in justice served for those connected to Her who are wrongfully accused. Syn gives us the power and will to say "no" when our boundaries, physical, emotional, and psychic, are under attack. I always call upon Syn to ward my home, my loved ones, and sacred space when we perform any rite I hold. For me, Syn is very much a goddess for the Me Too movement who helps guard boundaries and protect those who have been raped or fear sexual, other physical violence, or emotional abuse. Anyone who needs warding can call upon her.

> Hail Syn!
> Vigilant Warden of Boundaries,
> Help me safeguard boundaries
> Both seen and unseen.
> Give me the wit and will to say "No"
> When I must!
> Instill in me the courage and might
> to shut the door
> to baneful folk and baneful energies.
> Guard me
> as I open doors, long closed, within myself
> that no secrets lurk like intruders.
> May I welcome truth—
> even a hard truth—
> and dismiss that which no longer serves my growth
> so that I may know myself.

Ward me well
as I cross boundaries and make choices
that lead me to new paths, fords, and territories in my life.
May I be courageous and say "No! Enough!"
and take action
when my right to life, liberty, and happiness
is threatened.
Guard all those whose boundaries have been shattered
By violence, oppressions, and sickness.
May we be vigilant wardens of our bodies!

Lady of Righteous Refusal
Help me to become a wise and strong warden
Of my life's garths
That they may be filled with frith and freedom.
  —Maire Durkan

Symbol: Sword, birch broom.

Runes: Elhaz, ᛉ (the elk sedge—great rune of warding); Isa, ᛁ (rune of stasis, form, solidity—nothing moves until the ice melts).

Hlín—The Protectress (The Offense)

I like to think that I'm a pretty congenial person, but there are times when I go on the offensive, charging ahead with words and deeds to defend my "cubs" if the need is dire. While Hlín and Syn complement each other and work together in the work of protection, Syn stands before the doors of the keep defending its boundaries while Hlín is in the field, like a first responder; her protective energy is offensive, like a mama bear's. Her name, which means "protector," is also used as a kenning for Frigg in *Völuspá* (52) when her monumental attempts to turn Baldr's wyrd fail and when the seeress predicts that she will be unable to save Odin from Fenrir at Ragnarök.

Snorri says of Hlín that she "is appointed to guard over people whom Frigg wishes to protect from danger. From her name comes the expression that he who escapes finds *hleiner* [peace and quiet]" (Byock 2005, p. 43). Those fleeing violence, oppression, and those wounded by grief and physical and emotional hurt can call out to her for refuge and protection. My experience of Hlín is that she is the quintessential cool woman in a crisis. Some may find her cold and aloof, but that is not really the case. She is focused, always assessing and acting in the ways that are most needed to ensure that her charge is safe and stable. She is knowledgeable, competent, and controlled in situations that are often hostile and tense. But, like all species of mama bears, she has great empathy for the ones she must protect, and will charge in with force to rescue Frigg's dear ones.

> I raise a horn to Hlín!
> Mighty Protectress,
> Shield us and help up prepare
> Havens from all harm!
>
> Stand before refugees and
> Fugitives fleeing violence and strife
> And guide them to safe havens.
>
> Inspire us to act wisely,
> work with our legislators,
> and welcome refugees
> fleeing the horrors of war
> the horrors of abuse
> the horrors of oppression!
> Giver of solace,
> ease our troubles
> and dry our tears
> that we may find peace
> and joy in our lives.
> —Maire Durkan

Symbol: Shield.

Runes: Elhaz, Y (great rune of protection); Kenaz, < (the torch for light and guidance); Sowilo, ꤛ (victory); Berkano, ꃃ (shelter, protection, nurturing).

Snotra (Sno-trah)—The Lady of Etiquette

> Manners are a sensitive awareness of the feelings of others. If you have that awareness, you have good manners, no matter what fork you use.
> —Emily Post

Somewhere around the age of four (certainly before I entered kindergarten), my parents made very sure that when an adult friend or relative offered me something, I should respond with *"yesplease"* or *"nothanks."* For much of my early childhood I considered those small courtesies to be one word. My kindergarten teacher kept up the good fight by reading us Gelett Burgess's *Goops* poems—which made a lasting impression as I often quoted them to my own children. So, at a tender age I learned that being polite will open doors and raise a smile. While that's not always the case, etiquette is the frithy oil that keeps the wheels of society turning smoothly and Snotra (ON "the clever one") is Frigg's designated patroness of etiquette. Snotra presides over the varying and intricate web of rules that govern good behavior within social groups and societies. Although etiquette in the past enforced social codes and status (and in some societies—like Theodish society—still does), today's etiquette is focused on treating people with consideration and respect so that one can establish frithful interactions and relationships. Understanding the customs and etiquette of a society can mean the difference between causing insult and injury and creating positive, functional relationships. Snorri calls Snotra "wise and courtly," and says that "from her name comes the custom of calling a clever woman or man *snotr*" (Byock, 2005, p. 43). Snotra can also guide us in our knowledge of Heathen ways and customs and help us to adapt them to our time and place.

126

Hail Snotra!
Wise Lady of Etiquette
As I navigate the customs
Of groups and gatherings
Grant me the gift
Of courteous words and deeds
And the patience, perseverance, and open-mindedness
I will need to learn customs and courtesy
That I may build bridges of frith and friendship.
Inspire my words with warmth and wisdom
And may I act as your agent!
Hail Snotra!
    —Maire Durkan

Symbol: Linen handkerchief.

Runes: Fehu, ᚠ (success and happiness); Wunjo, ᚹ (joy, comfort, harmony); Ehwaz, ᛗ (teamwork, trust, loyalty); Mannaz, ᛗ (attitude towards others and their attitude towards you); Othala, ᛟ (heritage, group order, group prosperity).

Gná—The Messenger

More than one thousand eight hundred miles in ten days! Before the telephone or telegraph had made their appearance, the Pony Express could deliver a letter faster than ever before. Now we deliver messages in less than an eye blink anywhere in the world and even into space. But we are still stuck within the constraints of linear time. For Gná, however, time flows differently. Like all of the Great Ones, she exists outside of our specific point in time, and is therefore a handy companion for meditation, seidr, and any kind of trance work that takes you to other planes of existence. Gná is Frigg's messenger, and she provides us with a way to communicate with Frigg and the other gods and goddesses. Snorri tells us that Frigg sends Gná on errands "to different worlds." She rides Hofvarpnir [Hoof Kicker] which, like Odin's Sleipnir, carries her over land and sea. He states that "From Gná's name comes the custom of saying that something *gnæfir* [looms] when it rises up high" (Byock, 2005, p. 44). She soars above and beyond the restrictions of time and space, and can help us soar beyond our limitations to attain our true potential. She appears to me with a slim runner's physique and possesses an energetic, sparkling energy.

Frigg's Fleet Lady,
On Hofvarpnir hasten
Across the worlds
with divine messages!
Lift me over limitations
Teach me to fare forth fearlessly
Into the realm of spirit
And return rich in wisdom.
May my messages of love and devotion
Reach All-Mother Frigg
And Her shining circle of frith!
Hail Gná!
—Maire Durkan

Symbol: A horse.

Runes: Ehwaz, ᛗ (transportation and communication between the worlds); Eiwaz, ᛁ (enlightenment, endurance); Raidho, ᚱ (journeying), Ansuz, ᚠ (communication, insight, power of words).

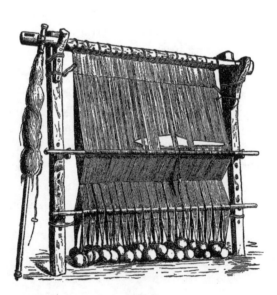

Bibliography

"*Pri-." *Etymology Online*, www.etymonline.com/word/*pri-.

Ashliman, D. L. "Merseburg Incantations." *Merseburg Incantations*, University of Pittsburgh, 23 Sept. 1998. www.pitt.edu/~dash/merseburg.html .

Byock, Jesse L. *The Prose Edda*. Penguin, 2005.

Davidson, Hilda Roderick Ellis. *Gods and Myths of Northern Europe*. Penguin Books, 1969.

Davidson, Hilda Ellis. *Roles of the Northern Goddess*. Routledge, 2005.

Dreams Sung True | Chant Albums From The Assembly of the Sacred Wheel, Assembly of the Sacred Wheel, www.sacredwheel.org/dream/dreams-sung-true.html.

Durkan, Maire B. "The Role of Örlög, Sköp and Urðr in the Vengeance of Guðrún Gjúkadóttir." *Idunna: A Journal of Northern Tradition*, 2018, pp. 19–23.

Foulke, William Dudley. *History of the Langobards*. Universiy of Pennsylvania Press, 1974.

Gundarsson, Kveldulf. *Our Troth*. BookSurge, 2007.

Gundarsson, Kveldulf. *The Teutonic Way*. The Three Little Sisters LLC, 2019.

Heaney, Seamus, and Daniel Donoghue. *Beowulf: a Verse Translation*. W.W. Norton and Company, 2000.

Hodge, Winifred. "On the Meaning of Frith." Frigga's Web Association, www.friggasweb.org/frith.html.

Karlsdóttir Alice. *Norse Goddess Magic: Trancework, Mythology, and Ritual*. Destiny Books, 2015.

Lafayllve, Patricia M. *A Practical Heathen's Guide to Asatru*. Llewellyn Publications, 2013.

Larrington, Carolyne. *The Poetic Edda*. Oxford University Press, 2014.

Lindow, John. *Norse Mythology: A Guide to the Gods, Heroes, Rituals, and Beliefs*. Oxford University Press, 2002.

Orchard, Andy. *Dictionary of Norse Myth and Legend*. Cassell, 1997.

Paxson, Diana L. *Essential Asatru: Walking the Path of Norse Paganism*. Citadel, 2007.

Paxson, Diana. "Beloved: On Frigg and Her Handmaidens." *Hrafnar*, hrafnar.org/articles/dpaxson/asynjur/frigg/ .

Scudder, Bernard. "Egil's Saga." *The Sagas of the Icelanders*, pp. 152–153.

Simek, Rudolf, and Angela Hall. *Dictionary of Northern Mythology*. D.S. Brewer, 2007.

Smiley, Jane. *The Sagas of the Icelanders*. Penguin, 2005.

Sturluson, Snorri. *Heimskringla, or The Lives of the Norse Kings*. Academic Press, 1990.

"Women in the Viking Age." *National Museum of Denmark*, en.natmus. dk/historical-knowledge/denmark/prehistoric-period-until-1050-ad/ the-viking-age/the-people/women/.

About The Author

Maire Durkan is a Friggswoman, an ordained Godsperson and Delaware steward for The Troth, and a witch in the Assembly of the Sacred Wheel tradition. Her spiritual work is deeply informed by her connection to deity, ancestors, and weal-working wights, and is deeply rooted in both of her spiritual traditions. She is also a children's book author, poet, teacher, and birth and postpartum doula. She lives with her amazing husband Patrick (of 37 years), the youngest contingent of their nine children, a trio of spoiled felines, and four pet chickens, near the beautiful Brandywine River Valley of Northern Delaware.

The Troth is an international organization that brings together many paths and traditions within Germanic Heathenry, such as Ásatrú, Theodish Belief, Urglaawe, Forn Sed, and Anglo-Saxon Heathenry. We welcome all who have been called to follow the elder ways of Heathenry, and who have heard the voices of the Gods and Goddesses of Heathenry, our ancestors, the landvættir, and the spirits around us.

To find out more about our organization or to join us, visit **http://www. thetroth.org/**, contact us at **troth-questions@thetroth.org**, or look for us on Facebook at **https://www.facebook.com/groups/TheTroth/**

Our complete line of books and back issues of our journal *Idunna* may be viewed at **https://www.lulu.com/spotlight/thetroth**

For book reviews, interviews, or any other matters connected with our publications, please contact us at **troth-shope@thetroth.org**